Type 2 Diabetes Cookbook for Beginners

1800 days Authentic, Delicious, and Easy-to-Prepare Recipes for a Balanced Life with Type 2 Diabetes | Including a 30-Day Meal Plan to Transform Your Health and Overcome Your Deepest Food Fears.

Clara Erickson

Table of Content

Chapter 1: Introduction

In an ever-evolving world, where the pulse of science and the heartbeat of human experience intersect, the narrative of Type 2 diabetes unfolds. It's not merely a medical condition defined by numbers and charts; it's a lived journey, textured by daily choices, challenges, and triumphs. At its core, it's a story about people – their battles, their resilience, and their ever-present quest for balance. And like any profound tale, this one too has its heroes: knowledge, understanding, and, intriguingly, the plates on our dining tables. This book delves deep into this multifaceted world, shedding light on the essence of Type 2 diabetes, the pivotal role nutrition plays in its tapestry, and the empowering tools at our disposal. We embark on a voyage, not just through the corridors of medical wisdom but also through the alleys of everyday experiences, savoring the flavors, textures, and nuances that make the narrative of Type 2 diabetes uniquely profound.

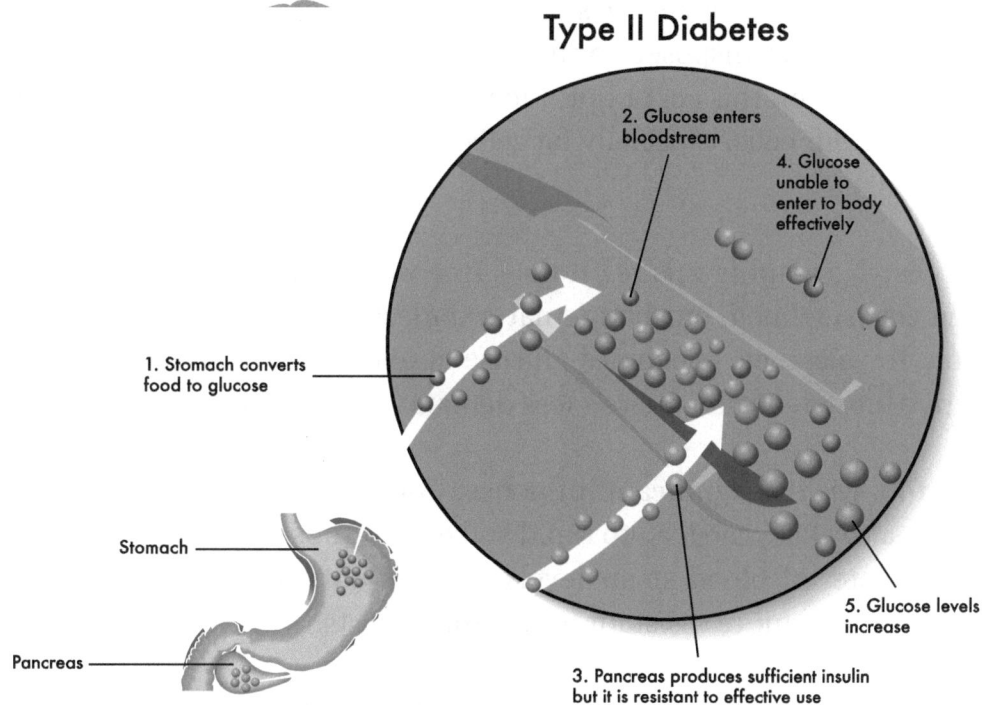

Type II Diabetes

1. Stomach converts food to glucose

2. Glucose enters bloodstream

4. Glucose unable to enter to body effectively

Stomach

Pancreas

5. Glucose levels increase

3. Pancreas produces sufficient insulin but it is resistant to effective use

The World of Type 2 Diabetes

What is Type 2 Diabetes?

In the mosaic of health challenges the world grapples with, Type 2 diabetes stands out as one of the most prominent pieces. But what exactly is it? At its core, Type 2 diabetes is a long-term metabolic disorder that affects how your body metabolizes sugar. While that might sound straightforward, the layers of this condition are intricate and multifaceted.

Imagine your body as a complex factory. One of the primary products it manufactures is a type of sugar called glucose, which serves as a primary energy source for our cells. This glucose travels around in our bloodstream, waiting for an invite into the cells where it can be put to work. The invite, in this case, is provided by a hormone called insulin, which our pancreas produces. Think of insulin as the key that unlocks the door to our cells, letting glucose in.

Now, in the world of Type 2 diabetes, something goes awry with this invitation system. It's not that the body doesn't produce insulin; it does. But for various reasons, the cells become resistant to it. They no longer open their doors as readily to glucose, even when insulin is trying to usher it in. As a result, glucose accumulates in the blood, leading to high blood sugar levels. Over time, if unchecked, this can wreak havoc on our health, affecting organs, nerves, and blood vessels.

But what causes this resistance to insulin in the first place? The answers to this question are like threads woven into a tapestry of genetics, lifestyle, and environment. While genes set the stage, making some of us more predisposed to insulin resistance, lifestyle choices play a major role in whether the curtains rise on this act or not. Elements like obesity, especially excess fat in the belly area, are top culprits. Our cells, especially fat cells in overweight people, become more resistant to the effects of insulin.

Our sedentary lifestyles amplify this resistance. In a world dominated by screens, where physical movement often gets sidelined, our body's natural mechanism of using glucose gets disrupted. A muscle in action, for instance, consumes glucose at about 20 times the rate of a muscle at rest. Hence, an inactive lifestyle means there's less demand for glucose, leading to its accumulation.

Dietary choices, too, wield a significant influence. Consuming highly processed foods, those rich in sugars and unhealthy fats, can lead to rapid spikes and subsequent crashes in blood sugar. Over time, this roller-coaster of blood sugar levels can tire out the pancreas, the insulin-producing organ, and make our cells more resistant to insulin's effects.

Let's paint a picture with an analogy. Imagine a town where every household loves to order pizza. There's one popular pizzeria, and it's working overtime to send out deliveries. Over time, as people keep ordering more and more pizzas, the delivery drivers (representing insulin) struggle to get the pizzas (glucose) to each house. The houses (cells) have had so many pizzas that they start refusing them, even when the drivers knock on the doors with more. The streets become congested with undelivered pizzas, just as the blood gets saturated with unused glucose.

Beyond the direct physiological components, there are environmental factors. Chronic stress, for instance, can elevate cortisol levels, a hormone that, in excess, can make cells more insulin resistant. Even disrupted sleep patterns can meddle with insulin's ability to function efficiently.

In navigating this ocean of information, one might ask, "How does one distinguish between Type 1 and Type 2 diabetes?" While both deal with disruptions in the body's handling of glucose and insulin, they stem from different roots. Type 1 diabetes is an autoimmune condition where the body's immune system mistakenly attacks insulin-producing cells in the pancreas. It's a case of mistaken identity, where the body inadvertently sabotages itself. On the other hand, Type 2, as we've explored, revolves around the body's response to insulin.

In shedding light on Type 2 diabetes, we peel back the layers of a condition that is as much a product of our modern world as it is of our biology. It's a testament to the interplay between our genes and the environment we craft around ourselves. As we journey through the understanding of this condition, remember that knowledge is the first step towards empowerment. Understanding Type 2 diabetes is the foundation on which proactive steps towards managing and possibly reversing it can be built.

The Importance of Proper Nutrition

In the theater of life, where our daily routines play out like acts in a drama, the food we consume takes center stage. Nutrition is not merely about satiating hunger or tantalizing our taste buds. It is an ongoing dialogue between our bodies and the environment, a delicate dance of nourishing and being nourished. For those touched by the shadow of Type 2 diabetes, this dialogue becomes especially profound, reminding us how closely our health is tethered to the sustenance we offer our bodies.

Imagine, if you will, our bodies as verdant gardens. Each cell, organ, and system represents a different plant, shrub, or tree. Like all gardens, ours requires diligent care and proper nourishment. Now, imagine pouring a liter of soda on a delicate rose or feeding a blooming orchid with sugary doughnuts. Sounds ludicrous, right? However, when we make poor nutritional choices, especially in the context of Type 2 diabetes, it's akin to subjecting our internal gardens to such illogical treatments.

When we discuss nutrition in the realm of Type 2 diabetes, we're delving into more than just the science of macronutrients and micronutrients. We are venturing into the art of balance, the wisdom of moderation, and the power of intentionality. It's not merely about "eating right." It's about forging a compassionate, understanding relationship with our bodies.

You've probably heard the saying, "You are what you eat." It might sound clichéd, but it holds a nugget of truth, especially for those managing Type 2 diabetes. The foods we consume have a direct bearing on our blood sugar levels. But it's not just about sugar. The matrix of nutrition for diabetics is a harmonious blend of understanding carbohydrates, proteins, fats, and how they converse with our internal systems.

Picture carbohydrates as the charismatic leaders of the food world. They're energetic, they get things moving, and they're often the life of the party. When digested, most carbohydrates break down into glucose, which, as we've already discussed, is a primary energy source for our cells. But not all carbohydrates wear the same cloak. While some release glucose rapidly into the bloodstream, causing a surge in blood sugar, others do so more gradually, offering a steady stream of energy. The art lies in distinguishing between these and making choices that favor the latter.

Fats and proteins, on the other hand, are the stabilizing forces in our dietary ensemble. Think of them as the grounding, wise elders of the nutrition tribe. They slow down the absorption of glucose, offering a buffer against rapid spikes in blood sugar. But, just like with carbohydrates, all fats aren't created equal. The secret is in discerning the allies from the foes, the avocados from the trans fats.

In the vast tapestry of diets and dietary advice that populates our modern world, it's easy to get lost. From keto to paleo, vegan to Mediterranean, the choices can be dizzying. But at the heart of proper nutrition, especially in the context of Type 2 diabetes, is a simple, timeless truth – wholesomeness. Fresh, unprocessed, and balanced meals are the cornerstones.

Let's voyage into a scene, shall we? Picture a sunlit kitchen, where fresh vegetables and fruits sprawl on the counter, their colors vibrant, their aromas inviting. There's a pot simmering with lentils, its earthy scent wafting through. A skillet sizzles with olive oil, where lean chicken turns golden. On another burner, quinoa dances in boiling water, its tiny grains promising a bite of nutty goodness. This isn't a scene from a gourmet restaurant. It's a snapshot of what proper nutrition can look like for someone managing Type 2 diabetes – fresh, diverse, and delightful.

However, it's also crucial to understand that this journey isn't about deprivation. It's about discovery. It's about rediscovering the joys of flavors in their purest forms, unmasked by excessive sugars and unhealthy fats. It's about the adventure of experimenting with spices, herbs, and textures to create meals that nourish both the body and soul.

It's worth noting, however, that this isn't a one-size-fits-all affair. Just as each of us has unique fingerprints, our nutritional needs and responses can vary. Factors like age, activity levels, metabolism, and even the nuances of our gut microbiome play roles in determining what works best. Hence, it's vital to adopt an approach of curiosity, listening to our bodies, and adjusting our sails based on how the winds of our health blow.

For someone peering into the world of Type 2 diabetes, it might seem daunting at first. It's a world where every meal, snack, and beverage choice carries weight. But, with the compass of proper nutrition, navigating becomes easier. It becomes an exploration, a daily act of self-love, and a testament to the resilience of the human spirit.

As we meander through the chapters of our lives, let's remember that each meal is a verse, each bite a word, and each flavor a sentiment. For those touched by Type 2 diabetes, proper nutrition is the poetry that makes the narrative not just survivable, but truly, deeply livable.

How to Manage Type 2 Diabetes Without Medications

In the heart of a vast forest, trees stand tall, their roots entwined deep beneath the soil. Their silent strength and enduring resilience serve as metaphors for those navigating the complex landscape of Type 2 diabetes. With its web of challenges, this condition can sometimes seem as tangled as the intricate root systems of the ancient trees. But there's hope, whispered through the leaves, a message that it's possible to manage, and even thrive, without relying solely on medications. It's a dance of discipline, understanding, and balance.

Imagine, for a moment, that our bodies are like orchestras. Each section — from strings to brass, woodwinds to percussion — must play in harmony for the melody of health to ring true. When one section falters, the entire symphony is affected. In the context of Type 2 diabetes, the rhythm of insulin and glucose often loses its synchronicity. And while medications can serve as a conductor to restore the balance, there are other maestros available, wielding batons of lifestyle choices, that can lead our body's orchestra with equal finesse.

The foremost of these maestros is physical activity. In a world dominated by screens and sedentary lifestyles, moving our bodies can seem like an arduous task. But it doesn't have to be an Olympic endeavor. The simple act of walking, like a soft violin playing in the background, can have profound effects. When muscles contract during physical activity, they actively consume glucose, independent of insulin's influence. It's as if the muscles are whispering to glucose, inviting it in, thereby helping maintain blood sugar balance. Over time, regular physical activity can also boost insulin sensitivity, ensuring that the symphony between insulin and glucose remains harmonious.

If walking is the violin, then stress management techniques, like meditation and deep breathing, are the soothing flutes. Chronic stress is like an out-of-tune trumpet in our body's orchestra, leading to elevated blood sugar levels due to the release of stress hormones. Techniques that foster relaxation, grounding, and mindfulness can retune this trumpet, ensuring that it complements rather than disrupts the melody of health. Envision yourself seated by a tranquil lake, its waters mirroring the azure sky, ripples creating patterns of serenity. This is the peace that effective stress management can bring, fortifying the fortresses against the onslaught of Type 2 diabetes.

Next in our orchestra is the cello of sleep. Its deep, resonant notes remind us of the importance of rest. A consistent sleep schedule, where the body rejuvenates in the embrace of slumber, can do wonders for blood sugar management. It's during these restful hours that the body orchestrates various repairs, ensuring that the instruments of our physiological systems remain in prime condition. Inconsistent or inadequate sleep can, over time, throw our insulin sensitivity out of whack. Hence, prioritizing a good night's sleep isn't just about feeling refreshed the next day; it's about ensuring the consistent cadence of our body's intricate symphony.

The vibrant drums of community and support can't be overlooked. Humans, by nature, are social creatures. Sharing our challenges and triumphs, our highs and lows, with a supportive community can offer emotional bolstering. Whether it's joining a group dedicated to physical activities, participating in support groups, or merely engaging in heartfelt conversations with loved ones, the strength of the collective can be a potent tool in managing Type 2 diabetes. Like the strong, consistent beat of drums, a supportive community provides the rhythm and backbone to our efforts.

Lastly, regular health check-ups play the role of the attentive audience, providing feedback, appreciation, and sometimes, constructive criticism. While this journey focuses on managing without medications, it's vital to have medical professionals in the loop. They serve as the discerning ears, attuned to the subtle nuances of our body's symphony, guiding us, and making tweaks when necessary.

In this grand concert of life, Type 2 diabetes might seem like an unwanted dissonance. But with the right maestros leading the way, it's possible to weave this dissonance into the larger melody, creating a piece that's not just about survival, but about thriving, dancing, and celebrating the music of existence.

As we stand at the edge of this forest of challenges, let us remember the trees, with their deep roots and tall canopies. They whisper tales of endurance, of bending with the wind but never breaking, of drawing sustenance from the earth and reaching for the skies. Their lesson is clear: with the right tools, strategies, and mindset, it's possible to manage Type 2 diabetes, not with resignation, but with fervor, passion, and a zest for life.

To navigate this journey is to embrace every note, every beat, and every rhythm that life offers, turning challenges into melodies, obstacles into harmonies, and every setback into a stepping stone towards a brighter, healthier tomorrow.

Having explored the intricacies of Type 2 diabetes, from its foundational understanding to its nuanced management without medications, it becomes evident that our day-to-day choices, particularly those on our plates, carry monumental significance. In the dance of glucose and insulin, where every misstep can echo through our system, it is imperative to equip ourselves with the knowledge of foods that serve as allies and those that might be foes in disguise. Our plates, after all, aren't just canvases of culinary artistry, but battlegrounds where the fight for health and balance is constantly waged. As we stand at this juncture, poised to delve deeper into the dietary aspect of managing diabetes, we should appreciate the gravity of our dietary choices. Every bite we take has a story to tell, every flavor carries a message, and every meal presents an opportunity. With this foundation laid, let's journey into the realm of diet and Type 2 diabetes, starting with an exploration of foods we should embrace with open arms and those we might consider approaching with caution. The table is set, and it's time to discover the symphony of sustenance that awaits.

Understanding and Managing Diabetes through Diet

Foods to Prefer and Those to Avoid

In the vast tapestry of human culinary art, there's a myriad of choices. Every dish, every ingredient, tells a tale, not just of flavor, but of health, tradition, and identity. When we talk about Type 2 diabetes, this narrative undergoes a transformation. It becomes a story of understanding, adaptation, and a celebration of the harmony between taste and well-being.

Imagine, for a moment, a bustling marketplace somewhere deep in the heartlands of America. The sun is a golden orb in the sky, casting its glow on stalls brimming with produce. The air is punctuated with the tantalizing aroma of fresh herbs, the sweet scent of ripe fruits, and the earthy fragrance of vegetables plucked straight from Mother Earth's bosom. Every item in this market carries a message, a subtle whisper, guiding those with Type 2 diabetes toward choices that nurture and heal.

At the heart of this marketplace stands a stall with a rainbow array of fruits and vegetables. Vibrant red tomatoes, sun-kissed oranges, verdant greens, and rich purples, it's a visual feast. These fresh produce items are nature's gifts to those aiming to manage diabetes through diet. They're packed with fiber, antioxidants, vitamins, and minerals. But more than their nutritional profile, they represent the foods to be embraced with open arms. A succulent berry or a crisp apple is not just a fruit; it's a testament to the power of nature's pharmacy.

However, as you drift deeper into the market, there's a corner shrouded in shadows, representing foods that need cautious approach. Here, amidst the hazy fog, lie processed foods. Laden with additives, sugars, and unhealthy fats, they whisper seductive promises of convenience and taste. But for someone with Type 2 diabetes, these are sirens that can lead one astray. The white breads, sugary beverages, processed meats, and snack foods might seem like benign treats, but they carry the potential to disrupt the intricate dance of blood sugar levels.

Then there's the lane of grains. Quinoa, barley, and oats sing songs of ancient civilizations, of cultures that understood the power of complex carbohydrates. They release glucose slowly, ensuring a steady and controlled energy supply. In contrast, refined grains, stripped of their bran and germ, rush into the bloodstream like a river in spate, causing rapid spikes in blood sugar.

Amidst the symphony of this marketplace, the aroma of fresh fish wafts in the air. Salmon, mackerel, and sardines are like the poets of the sea, rich in omega-3 fatty acids, singing tales of heart health and reduced inflammation. But in the shadowy alleyways, lurk their counterparts - the deep-fried temptations and fatty meats. They, with their high saturated fat content, are the balladeers of caution, warning of potential harm to heart and blood vessels.

The tales don't end here. The marketplace is also home to the enchanting world of legumes. Beans, lentils, and chickpeas are like age-old storytellers, narrating epics of fiber, protein, and a low glycemic index. They are the allies in the quest for blood sugar management. Yet, lurking nearby are the sugary desserts and candies, like trickster spirits, tempting with their sweetness but often leading one into the treacherous terrains of high blood sugar.

At the edge of this marketplace, stands a humble stall, brimming with nuts and seeds. Almonds, walnuts, and flaxseeds, with their heart-healthy fats and protein, are like the wise old sages, guiding one towards satiety and health. Their message is clear: in moderation, they can be potent tools in the arsenal against Type 2 diabetes.

As the day winds down, and the golden orb of the sun dips below the horizon, the marketplace, with its myriad of choices, leaves us with a profound realization. The journey of managing diabetes through diet is not about deprivation. It's about discernment. It's about understanding the stories that foods tell, the promises they make, and the cautions they whisper.

It's about savoring the sweetness of a ripe berry, the crunch of a fresh vegetable, and the richness of a piece of salmon, all the while knowing that with each bite, one is taking a step towards health. It's about avoiding the sirens of processed foods, not out of fear, but out of love for oneself.

And as the stars twinkle overhead, one thing becomes crystal clear: the landscape of dietary choices for someone with Type 2 diabetes is as vast and varied as the tapestry of human culinary art itself. It's a celebration, a dance, and most importantly, a journey of love, understanding, and harmony.

Balancing Carbohydrates, Proteins, and Fats

In the grand theater of nutrition, three characters stand out with unparalleled prominence: Carbohydrates, Proteins, and Fats. These are not mere molecular compounds; they are protagonists of our dietary narrative, each playing a distinct role, each holding the key to the delicate ballet of our body's physiology, especially for those who dance to the rhythm of Type 2 diabetes.

Let's imagine, for a fleeting moment, the body as a grand orchestra, with every cell, tissue, and organ contributing its unique note. The fuel for this musical ensemble? The food we consume. And amidst this harmonious composition, carbohydrates, proteins, and fats are the three lead instrumentalists, setting the tone, pace, and depth of the melody.

The world of **carbohydrates** is as vast as it is misunderstood. To many, this macronutrient conjures images of sugar-laden desserts and starchy foods. But carbohydrates are not just about the quick energy spike and the inevitable crash. They are the wind instruments of our body's orchestra, producing the initial notes that set the melody in motion. Carbohydrates are the body's primary source of energy, but not all carbs are crafted alike. Complex carbohydrates, like whole grains and legumes, release glucose slowly into the bloodstream, ensuring a melodious and sustained tune, a gentle rise, and fall in the symphony of blood sugar levels. Simple sugars, however, are the erratic trumpets, causing a cacophony of rapid spikes and crashes. For the maestro managing Type 2 diabetes, understanding this distinction is pivotal. It's about choosing the serene flute over the boisterous trumpet, opting for the harmonious play of complex carbs.

Next, we encounter the powerful string section: **proteins**. If carbohydrates are the initial notes of our physiological melody, proteins are the consistent undertones, the steady hum that provides structure and depth. Proteins repair, rebuild, and rejuvenate. They are the building blocks of muscles, enzymes, and hormones. For someone with Type 2 diabetes, proteins play an instrumental role, literally and figuratively. They slow the absorption of glucose, ensuring that the body's melody doesn't spiral into discord. Consider the serenity of a cello's tune. It's deep, resonating, and grounding. That's the magic of proteins. Foods like lean meats, poultry, fish, tofu, and legumes are the cellos and violas of our dietary orchestra, ensuring the symphony remains harmonious and balanced.

And then, we have the percussion section, the backdrop against which the entire orchestra comes alive: **fats**. Often vilified, fats are, in fact, essential. They are the drums and timpani, providing the rhythm, the depth, the heartbeat of our body's concert. Fats cushion our organs, support cell growth, and are vital for absorbing certain nutrients. But again, the world of fats is nuanced. There's the gentle, rhythmic beat of unsaturated fats found in olive oil, nuts, and avocados. These fats, like a well-timed drum, support heart health and regulate blood sugar. Then there's the erratic, jarring clash of trans fats and saturated fats, which need to be approached with caution, like a drummer who's lost the rhythm.

It's this intricate interplay between carbohydrates, proteins, and fats that defines the magnum opus of our body's function. For those steering the ship of Type 2 diabetes, this balance is not just about numbers or ratios. It's an art. It's about listening intently to the orchestra, understanding when the wind instruments need to be mellowed, when the string section needs prominence, and when the drums need to be rhythmic and not overpowering.

Imagine crafting a meal where the complex carbs set the initial tune. A melody of whole grains, perhaps a sonnet of quinoa or an aria of barley. Then, the proteins join in, the resonating tunes of grilled chicken or the harmonious notes of lentils. And finally, the rhythm sets in, the gentle beat of avocado or the consistent pulse of olive oil.

For someone with Type 2 diabetes, this is not just a meal. It's a composition, a symphony of health, where every bite is a note, every flavor a chord, and every meal a masterpiece.

As our curtain draws to a close on this act, we realize that balancing carbohydrates, proteins, and fats is not a rigid science. It's a fluid art form, a dance, a song, a symphony. It's about understanding the roles, the nuances, the highs, and the lows of these three macronutrients. And for those with Type 2 diabetes, it's about conducting this orchestra with grace, wisdom, and a deep understanding of the music of nutrition.

Using Recipes as a Management Tool

In the realm of managing Type 2 diabetes, amidst the conversations on medications, workouts, and blood sugar readings, lies a powerful, yet often overlooked tool: recipes. Now, before we relegate this to just ingredients listed on a card or a mere blueprint for a meal, let's unfurl the tapestry of recipes and explore their transformative potential.

Imagine, if you will, a map. A beautiful, intricate map, dotted with landmarks, terrains, and paths. This map doesn't merely guide you from Point A to Point B; it narrates tales, unlocks secrets, and offers paths less traveled. Such is the power of a well-crafted recipe. It's not just about creating a dish; it's about charting a course through the intricate landscape of nutrition, savoring the journey, and reaching a destination that nourishes both the body and soul.

A recipe is a story, told in flavors and textures, aromas and colors. And for those with Type 2 diabetes, these stories become pivotal. They're tales of triumph, where dietary challenges transform into culinary masterpieces. They're sagas of discovery, where ingredients once deemed 'off-limits' become stars of the show. They're chronicles of balance, where carbohydrates, proteins, and fats dance in harmony, creating a symphony on the plate.

Yet, why are recipes such invaluable tools in the arsenal against Type 2 diabetes?

Firstly, recipes demystify the culinary canvas. For many, the kitchen can be an intimidating stage, with the pressure to craft meals that not only tantalize the taste buds but also align with dietary guidelines. Recipes, with their structured guidance and measured proportions, become the compass. They eliminate the guesswork, offering a reliable framework within which one can play, experiment, and innovate.

Take, for example, the alchemy of creating a hearty stew. For someone with Type 2 diabetes, the traditional recipe laden with starchy vegetables and sodium-rich broths may be a no-go. But armed with a recipe tailored for diabetes management, that same stew transforms. Suddenly, there's a bouquet of fiber-rich legumes, a symphony of low-glycemic vegetables, and a medley of herbs offering depth without the salt. The result? A dish that's a veritable mosaic of flavors, colors, and textures, all while being a steadfast ally in blood sugar management.

Secondly, recipes foster creativity. Yes, there are dietary guidelines to follow, certain foods to approach with caution, and others to embrace. But within these parameters lies a vast playground. Think of recipes as the gentle nudge, the whisper in the ear that says, "Why not try this?" They're the muse, inspiring one to see beyond the limitations and envision a world of culinary possibilities.

Recall a simple salad. In its basic form, it might be a medley of greens, a sprinkle of protein, and a dash of dressing. But through the lens of a curated recipe, this salad evolves. There's the crunch of toasted seeds, the burst of berries bursting with antioxidants, the silkiness of avocados rich in healthy fats, and the zing of a dressing crafted from cold-pressed oils and tangy vinegars. The salad is no longer just a side dish; it's the main event, a testament to the artistry recipes can usher in.

Lastly, recipes are anchors of consistency. In the journey of managing Type 2 diabetes, consistency in dietary choices is pivotal. Here, recipes become the lighthouse, guiding one safely through the tempestuous seas of dining decisions. With a trusted recipe in hand, there's clarity. There's assurance. One knows that the dish crafted will not only satiate the senses but also align with the overarching goals of health and wellness.

In essence, recipes are more than just culinary constructs. For those navigating the waters of Type 2 diabetes, they're companions, guides, and torchbearers. They transform the kitchen from a place of uncertainty to a sanctuary of discovery. They elevate dining from a mere act of sustenance to an experience of joy, exploration, and balance.

As we draw the curtains on this introductory chapter, it's essential to reflect on the kaleidoscope of insights and perspectives we've traversed. Type 2 diabetes, as we've come to appreciate, isn't a solitary note in the vast symphony of life. It's a complex melody, harmonizing medical wisdom with lived experience, challenges with solutions, and uncertainty with knowledge. The kitchen, often seen as a simple space of sustenance, emerges as a powerful stage where the drama of diabetes management plays out, with recipes as its script and ingredients as its characters. Yet, at its heart, the story remains deeply human. It's about us – our choices, our struggles, our victories. As we forge ahead into the subsequent chapters, let's carry forward the spirit of understanding, the commitment to balance, and the passion for life. For in the world of Type 2 diabetes, knowledge isn't just power; it's the beacon lighting the path to a healthier, more vibrant tomorrow.

Chapter 2: Recipes

Dive into the heart of the culinary realm tailored for individuals with Type 2 Diabetes. This chapter isn't just a compilation of dishes; it's a journey. Here, we've curated a selection of recipes that not only ensure proper nutrition but also indulge your taste buds with an array of flavors and textures. Food is one of life's greatest pleasures, and a diabetes diagnosis should not detract from that joy. Instead, it invites you to discover new ingredients, innovative cooking methods, and dishes that are as delightful as they are healthful. From energizing breakfasts to satiating desserts, each recipe has been crafted with two central tenets in mind: taste and health. As you flip through these pages, you'll find dishes inspired from around the globe, each providing a blend of rich tradition and modern twists, ensuring that every bite is a step toward better health without compromising on the soul of the dish.

Breakfast

Recipe 1: Quinoa Ambrosia with Blueberries

P.T.: 20 minutes
Ingr.: 1 cup al dente quinoa, ½ cup hand-picked blueberries, 1 tbsp chia granules, 1 tsp Ceylon cinnamon shards, ½ cup unsweetened almond nectar, 2 tbsp walnut nuggets.
Serves: 2
M. of C.: Stovetop alchemy

Process: In a copper cauldron, amalgamate quinoa with almond nectar. Elevate over a medium ember until tepid. Enfold in blueberries, chia granules, and cinnamon shards. Decant into ceramic vessels and besprinkle with walnut nuggets.
N.V.: Carbs: 35g, Protein: 8g, Fats: 9g, Fiber: 5g, Sugar: 7g.

Recipe 2: Florentine Egg Cloud with Feta Crumbles

P.T.: 15 minutes
Ingr.: 1 cup egg vapors, ½ cup chiffonade spinach, 2 tbsp feta morsels, 1 tsp EVOO droplets, pinch of pulverized noir peppercorn.
Serves: 1
M. of C.: Skillet fusion

Process: In a seasoned obsidian skillet, emanate EVOO. Incorporate spinach and sauté until languid. Admit egg vapors and let ensconce. Introduce feta and drape. Serve with peppercorn dust atop.
N.V.: Carbs: 4g, Protein: 28g, Fats: 7g, Fiber: 1g, Sugar: 2g.

Recipe 3: Almond Nectar & Chia Toast Elevation

Ingr.: 2 artisanal grain slabs, 2 tbsp almond nectar, 1 tbsp chia granules, 1 heirloom banana, thinly ringed.

Serves: 1

M. of C.: Ember-toasted

Process: Crisp grain slabs to a golden hue. Layer with almond nectar over each slab. Crown with banana circlets and sprinkle with chia granules.

N.V.: Carbs: 45g, Protein: 10g, Fats: 15g, Fiber: 8g, Sugar: 12g.

P.T.: 10 minutes

Recipe 4: Tofu Brekky Scramble Mirage

P.T.: 15 minutes

Ingr.: 1 block silken tofu, crumbled, 1 tsp turmeric flecks, 1 tsp EVOO droplets, 1/4 cup red bell pepper mosaics, 1/4 cup onion silvers, 2 tbsp nutritional yeast flakes.

Serves: 2

M. of C.: Skillet alchemy

Process: In an iron skillet, resonate EVOO, suffuse with pepper mosaics and onion silvers. Add tofu and turmeric, then amalgamate. Dust with yeast flakes before plating.

N.V.: Carbs: 9g, Protein: 20g, Fats: 9g, Fiber: 4g, Sugar: 3g.

Recipe 5: Avocado & Cottage Spread Delight

P.T.: 5 minutes

Ingr.: 1 ripened avocado, ¼ cup cottage cheese pearls, 1 tsp lemon zest filaments, sea salt granules to taste, 2 whole grain facades.

Serves: 1

M. of C.: Hand amalgamation

Process: Halve avocado and extricate flesh. Blend with cottage pearls, lemon zest, and salt. Slather on toasted grain facades.

N.V.: Carbs: 32g, Protein: 12g, Fats: 21g, Fiber: 10g, Sugar: 5g.

Recipe 6: Kale & Smoked Salmon Reveal

P.T.: 10 minutes

Ingr.: 1 cup kale fronds, 2 slices ethereal smoked salmon, 1 tsp caper baubles, 2 poached egg orbs.

Serves: 1

M. of C.: Tiered ensemble

Process: Lay kale on plate base, then drape with salmon. Garnish with caper baubles, then crown with egg orbs.

N.V.: Carbs: 3g, Protein: 25g, Fats: 11g, Fiber: 1g, Sugar: 0g.

Recipe 7: Ricotta Almond Pancake Surprise

P.T.: 15 minutes
Ingr.: 1 cup ricotta clusters, 2 tbsp almond meal, 1 egg, whisked into nebula, vanilla essences, a drop, 1 tsp coconut sugar crystals.
Serves: 2
M. of C.: Griddle dance

Process: Combine all elements into a harmonious blend. Ladle onto a heated griddle until bubbles form, then flip and brown the reverse side.
N.V.: Carbs: 8g, Protein: 12g, Fats: 15g, Fiber: 1g, Sugar: 4g.

Recipe 8: Sardine & Olive Tapenade Dawn

P.T.: 5 minutes
Ingr.: 4 sardine fillets, 2 tbsp Kalamata olives, crushed, 1 tsp EVOO droplets, zest of one lemon, 2 rustic bread silhouettes.
Serves: 2

M. of C.: Hand fusion
Process: Blend sardines, olives, EVOO, and zest. Spread over toasted bread silhouettes.
N.V.: Carbs: 25g, Protein: 15g, Fats: 18g, Fiber: 3g, Sugar: 2g.

Recipe 9: Chia & Macadamia Porridge Euphoria

P.T.: 20 minutes
Ingr.: 3 tbsp chia granules, 1 cup unsweetened almond nectar, 2 tbsp macadamia fragments, 1 tsp maple essence.
Serves: 1
M. of C.: Stovetop alchemy

Process: Fuse chia and almond nectar in a pot. Allow it to swell. Enrich with macadamia fragments and a drizzle of maple essence.
N.V.: Carbs: 18g, Protein: 7g, Fats: 21g, Fiber: 12g, Sugar: 4g.

Recipe 10: Green Spirulina Smoothie Dreamscape

P.T.: 5 minutes
Ingr.: 1 cup spinach, 1 tbsp spirulina powder, ½ avocado, 1 cup coconut water, 1 tsp honey nectar.
Serves: 1

M. of C.: Blender magic
Process: Introduce all ingredients into a blender, whirling into a velvety dreamscape.
N.V.: Carbs: 22g, Protein: 4g, Fats: 12g, Fiber: 8g, Sugar: 11g.

Recipe 11: Frittata Fusion with Zucchini Spirals

P.T.: 25 minutes
Ingr.: 3 cage-free egg orbs, 1 zucchini, spiraled, 2 tbsp feta crumbles, 1 tsp dill fronds, finely snipped, a hint of chili flakes.
Serves: 2

M. of C.: Oven reverie
Process: Whisk egg orbs, suffuse with dill, feta, and chili. Fold in zucchini spirals. Pour mixture into an oven-proof skillet, bake until set.

N.V.: Carbs: 7g, Protein: 14g, Fats: 9g, Fiber: 1g, Sugar: 4g.

Recipe 12: Turmeric Latte & Walnut-Butter Crescents

P.T.: 15 minutes
Ingr.: 2 cups almond nectar, 1 tsp turmeric dust, pinch of black pepper grains, 4 crescent rolls, 2 tbsp walnut butter spread.
Serves: 2
M. of C.: Stove simmer & oven caress

Process: Infuse almond nectar with turmeric and pepper, simmer till warm. Slather walnut spread on crescents, bake till golden.
N.V.: Carbs: 27g, Protein: 6g, Fats: 12g, Fiber: 3g, Sugar: 7g.

Recipe 13: Berries & Seed Medley Awe

P.T.: 10 minutes
Ingr.: 1 cup mixed berries, 2 tbsp pumpkin seeds, 2 tbsp sunflower kernels, drizzle of almond essence, 1 cup Greek yogurt, unsweetened.
Serves: 1

M. of C.: Chilled bowl merge
Process: Layer berries, seeds, and kernels in a bowl. Crown with Greek yogurt, then drizzle almond essence.
N.V.: Carbs: 25g, Protein: 19g, Fats: 12g, Fiber: 4g, Sugar: 14g.

Recipe 14: Artichoke & Pesto Omelet Hug

P.T.: 20 minutes
Ingr.: 3 egg orbs, 2 tbsp pesto ripples, 1 marinated artichoke heart, sliced, 1 tbsp Parmesan shavings.
Serves: 1
M. of C.: Skillet embrace

Process: Whisk egg orbs, integrate pesto. Pour into a skillet. Arrange artichoke slices. When nearly set, sprinkle Parmesan shavings.
N.V.: Carbs: 4g, Protein: 17g, Fats: 20g, Fiber: 1g, Sugar: 2g.

Recipe 15: Ginger-Melon Refresher Bowl

P.T.: 10 minutes
Ingr.: 1 cup cantaloupe balls, 1 tsp fresh ginger snippets, mint leaf coronets for garnish, squeeze of lime essence.
Serves: 1
M. of C.: Chilled merge

Process: In a frosted bowl, marinate melon with ginger snippets. Drizzle with lime essence. Crown with mint coronets.
N.V.: Carbs: 15g, Protein: 1g, Fats: 0.4g, Fiber: 1g, Sugar: 14g.

Recipe 16: Cacao-Chia Serenity Pudding

P.T.: 5 minutes (plus overnight chilling)

Ingr.: 3 tbsp chia granules, 1 cup almond nectar, 1 tbsp cacao powder, 1 tsp agave droplets, pinch of sea salt crystals.
Serves: 1
M. of C.: Refrigerator set

Process: Infuse chia granules with almond nectar, agave, cacao, and salt. Let it serenely set overnight in the chiller.
N.V.: Carbs: 35g, Protein: 7g, Fats: 11g, Fiber: 14g, Sugar: 12g.

Recipe 17: Miso Breakfast Soup Solace

P.T.: 15 minutes
Ingr.: 2 cups vegetable broth, 1 tbsp miso paste, 2 shiitake mushrooms, sliced, 1 green onion, snipped, tofu cubes.
Serves: 1
M. of C.: Stovetop serenity

Process: In a pot, warm broth. Integrate miso, mushrooms, onion, and tofu. Simmer until all elements are in solace.
N.V.: Carbs: 8g, Protein: 12g, Fats: 4g, Fiber: 2g, Sugar: 3g.

Recipe 18: Hazelnut & Pear Baked Divinity

P.T.: 30 minutes
Ingr.: 1 pear, cored, thinly sliced, 2 tbsp hazelnut butter, 1 tsp cinnamon haze, 1 tbsp honey rivulet.
Serves: 1
M. of C.: Oven glow

Process: In a ramekin, layer pear slices. Drizzle with hazelnut butter, honey, and sprinkle with cinnamon. Bake till tender.
N.V.: Carbs: 32g, Protein: 4g, Fats: 9g, Fiber: 6g, Sugar: 24g.

Recipe 19: Coconut & Cardamom Smoothie Veil

P.T.: 5 minutes
Ingr.: 1 cup coconut milk, 1 tsp cardamom whispers, 1 tbsp flaxseed particles, 1 date, pitted, and finely minced.
Serves: 1

M. of C.: Blender's embrace
Process: Introduce ingredients to a blender, whirl until the mixture wears a smooth veil.
N.V.: Carbs: 15g, Protein: 3g, Fats: 21g, Fiber: 4g, Sugar: 10g.

Recipe 20: Eggplant & Hummus Breakfast Torte

P.T.: 20 minutes
Ingr.: 1 small eggplant, thin circles, 3 tbsp hummus spread, 1 tsp za'atar sprinkling, 1 tbsp olive oil drizzles.
Serves: 1
M. of C.: Griddle & plate

Process: Griddle eggplant circles till tender. On a plate, stack with hummus between layers. Finish with za'atar and olive oil drizzles.
N.V.: Carbs: 23g, Protein: 5g, Fats: 13g, Fiber: 9g, Sugar: 11g.

Snacks and Starters

Recipe 1: Chickpea Crunch Bliss

P.T.: 40 minutes
Ingr.: 1 can chickpeas, 1 tsp paprika twirls, 2 tbsp olive oil mists.
Serves: 3-4
M. of C.: Oven crisping

Process: Toss chickpeas in paprika and olive oil. Roast until crunchy.
N.V.: Carbs: 22g, Protein: 7g, Fats: 5g, Fiber: 6g, Sugar: 4g.

Recipe 2: Beetroot Hummus Embrace

P.T.: 15 minutes
Ingr.: 1 beetroot, roasted, 2 tbsp tahini essence, 1 garlic clove, minced, squeeze of lemon zeal.
Serves: 4
M. of C.: Blender mesh
Process: Blend ingredients until silky. Serve chilled.
N.V.: Carbs: 9g, Protein: 3g, Fats: 8g, Fiber: 2g, Sugar: 5g.

Recipe 3: Zucchini Roll-Ups Caress

P.T.: 20 minutes
Ingr.: 2 zucchinis, thinly sliced, 3 tbsp goat cheese whispers, 1 tsp dill wisps.
Serves: 4
M. of C.: Raw & fresh

Process: Slather goat cheese on zucchini slices, sprinkle dill, and roll up.
N.V.: Carbs: 3g, Protein: 2g, Fats: 4g, Fiber: 1g, Sugar: 2g.

Recipe 4: Avocado & Tuna Delight

P.T.: 10 minutes
Ingr.: 1 ripe avocado, halved, 3 oz tuna flakes, 1 tsp caper sprinklings, hint of lemon.
Serves: 2
M. of C.: Assembled allure

Process: Stuff avocado halves with tuna and capers, finish with a lemon hint.
N.V.: Carbs: 10g, Protein: 12g, Fats: 15g, Fiber: 7g, Sugar: 1g.

Recipe 5: Tomato Basil Soup Euphoria

P.T.: 30 minutes
Ingr.: 5 ripe tomatoes, 1 onion, minced, 1 garlic clove, 1 tsp fresh basil murmur.
Serves: 2
M. of C.: Pot fusion

Process: Sauté onion & garlic. Add tomatoes, simmer. Blend until smooth, garnish with basil.
N.V.: Carbs: 14g, Protein: 2g, Fats: 0.5g, Fiber: 3g, Sugar: 8g.

Recipe 6: Quinoa Spinach Munchies

P.T.: 45 minutes
Ingr.: 1 cup cooked quinoa, 1/2 cup spinach, wilted, 2 tbsp feta, crumbled, 1 egg orb.
Serves: 12 munchies
M. of C.: Oven's embrace

Process: Combine ingredients, form small patties. Bake until golden.
N.V.: Carbs: 7g, Protein: 3g, Fats: 2g, Fiber: 1g, Sugar: 0.5g.

Recipe 7: Almond-Stuffed Dates Serenade

P.T.: 10 minutes
Ingr.: 10 dates, pitted, 10 almonds, roasted, 1 tsp coconut shreds.
Serves: 10
M. of C.: No-cook symphony

Process: Nestle an almond inside each date. Finish with a coconut sprinkle.
N.V.: Carbs: 17g, Protein: 1g, Fats: 1g, Fiber: 2g, Sugar: 15g.

Recipe 8: Lemon Garlic Olives Rhapsody

P.T.: 5 minutes (plus marinating time)
Ingr.: 1 cup green olives, 1 garlic clove, minced, 1 lemon zest twirl.
Serves: 4
M. of C.: Marinate and savor

Process: Infuse olives with garlic and lemon zest. Allow flavors to meld.
N.V.: Carbs: 1g, Protein: 0g, Fats: 5g, Fiber: 0.5g, Sugar: 0g.

Recipe 9: Spiced Edamame Symphony

P.T.: 10 minutes
Ingr.: 1 cup edamame, 1 tsp chili flakes, hint of sea salt crystals.
Serves: 2
M. of C.: Pan-seared rhythm

Process: Sear edamame with chili flakes. Season with salt. Serve warm.
N.V.: Carbs: 7g, Protein: 8g, Fats: 4g, Fiber: 3g, Sugar: 2g.

Recipe 10: Pecan-Stuffed Figs Sonata

P.T.: 15 minutes
Ingr.: 5 figs, halved, 10 pecans, toasted, 1 tsp honey drizzle.
Serves: 5
M. of C.: Baking ballad

Process: Place a pecan on each fig half. Drizzle with honey. Bake briefly.
N.V.: Carbs: 8g, Protein: 0.5g, Fats: 2g, Fiber: 1.5g, Sugar: 7g.

Recipe 11: Herb-Infused Cottage Cheese Brilliance

P.T.: 10 minutes
Ingr.: 1 cup low-fat cottage cheese, 1 tsp chive snippets, 1 tsp dill morsels, a sprinkling of paprika dust.
Serves: 3

M. of C.: Ensemble of zest
Process: Mix cottage cheese with herbs. Crown with paprika. Refrigerate & relish.
N.V.: Carbs: 4g, Protein: 12g, Fats: 1g, Fiber: 0g, Sugar: 3g.

Recipe 12: Kale Chips Cascade

P.T.: 25 minutes
Ingr.: 1 bunch kale, torn, 1 tbsp olive oil droplets, sea salt whispers.
Serves: 4
M. of C.: Oven-fanned crispness

Process: Coat kale in olive oil, sprinkle with salt. Oven-crisp to perfection.
N.V.: Carbs: 7g, Protein: 3g, Fats: 4g, Fiber: 1g, Sugar: 0g.

Recipe 13: Tangy Tomato Bruschetta Overture

P.T.: 15 minutes
Ingr.: 5 cherry tomatoes, chopped, 1 garlic clove, minced, 1 tsp basil snippets, whole grain toast shards.
Serves: 5

M. of C.: Assembled delight
Process: Merge tomatoes, garlic, and basil. Mount atop toast shards. Serve immediately.
N.V.: Carbs: 10g, Protein: 2g, Fats: 1g, Fiber: 2g, Sugar: 2g.

Recipe 14: Pumpkin Seed Trail

P.T.: 10 minutes
Ingr.: 1 cup pumpkin seeds, a hint of cayenne sprinkle, sea salt murmurs.
Serves: 4
M. of C.: Pan-tossed journey

Process: Toast seeds till golden. Infuse with cayenne and salt. Relish the crunch.
N.V.: Carbs: 5g, Protein: 8g, Fats: 13g, Fiber: 2g, Sugar: 1g.

Recipe 15: Coconut & Almond Cluster Riddle

P.T.: 15 minutes
Ingr.: 1/2 cup unsweetened coconut ribbons, 1/4 cup almonds, crushed, 2 tbsp chia seeds, a touch of stevia.
Serves: 10 clusters

M. of C.: Refrigerated magic
Process: Combine ingredients. Mold into clusters. Chill and enjoy.
N.V.: Carbs: 4g, Protein: 2g, Fats: 9g, Fiber: 3g, Sugar: 1g.

Recipe 16: Tangy Ginger Turmeric Cubes

P.T.: 20 minutes (plus freezing)
Ingr.: 1-inch ginger, grated, 1 tsp turmeric twilight, 1 cup coconut water, stevia droplets.
Serves: 10 cubes
M. of C.: Frozen zest

Process: Blend all, pour into ice trays. Freeze. Enjoy as a chilling nibble.
N.V.: Carbs: 3g, Protein: 0.5g, Fats: 0g, Fiber: 0.2g, Sugar: 2g.

Recipe 17: Spinach & Feta Dip Drama

P.T.: 10 minutes
Ingr.: 1 cup spinach, wilted, 3 tbsp feta crumbles, 1 tbsp Greek yogurt swirls, garlic essence.
Serves: 4

M. of C.: Blender's ballet
Process: Whirl all in a blender. Serve cool.
N.V.: Carbs: 2g, Protein: 4g, Fats: 5g, Fiber: 1g, Sugar: 1g.

Recipe 18: Cucumber Melon Medley

P.T.: 10 minutes
Ingr.: 1 cucumber, sliced, 1/2 melon, scooped, 1 tbsp mint silvers.
Serves: 4
M. of C.: Fresh & cool

Process: Mix cucumber, melon, and mint. Serve as a refreshing starter.
N.V.: Carbs: 8g, Protein: 1g, Fats: 0.5g, Fiber: 1g, Sugar: 6g.

Recipe 19: Portobello Cap Delicacy

P.T.: 20 minutes
Ingr.: 2 Portobello mushrooms, 2 tbsp ricotta whisks, 1 tsp thyme strands, olive oil drizzles.
Serves: 2

M. of C.: Oven-baked
Process: Fill mushroom caps with ricotta and thyme. Bake till soft and luscious.
N.V.: Carbs: 5g, Protein: 8g, Fats: 7g, Fiber: 1.5g, Sugar: 2g.

Recipe 20: Beet Hummus Hues

P.T.: 15 minutes
Ingr.: 1 beetroot, boiled & chopped, 1 cup chickpeas, a tahini swirl, lemon zest.
Serves: 4
M. of C.: Blender's whirl

Process: Blend all to a smooth hummus. Enjoy with vegetable sticks.
N.V.: Carbs: 12g, Protein: 6g, Fats: 4g, Fiber: 4g, Sugar: 3g.

Meat

Beef

Recipe 1: Basil Beef Brocade

P.T.: 20 minutes
Ingr.: 200g lean beef strips, basil webbing, 2 tsp olive oil, garlic wisp.
Serves: 2
M. of C.: Pan-seared

Process: Sauté garlic, add beef. Once browned, incorporate basil. Serve hot.
N.V.: Carbs: 0g, Protein: 22g, Fats: 9g, Fiber: 0g, Sugar: 0g.

Recipe 2: Spiced Beef Latticework

P.T.: 25 minutes
Ingr.: 200g beef cubes, a pinch of cumin dust, coriander essence, salt murmur.
Serves: 2
M. of C.: Oven-roasted

Process: Marinate beef with spices. Roast to perfection. Relish with veggies.
N.V.: Carbs: 1g, Protein: 23g, Fats: 10g, Fiber: 0.5g, Sugar: 0g.

Recipe 3: Beef & Broccoli Ballet

P.T.: 30 minutes
Ingr.: 150g lean beef slivers, broccoli florets, soy sauce trace, ginger strands.
Serves: 2
M. of C.: Wok-tossed
Process: Sear beef, mix with broccoli. Drizzle soy sauce, add ginger. Toss.
N.V.: Carbs: 8g, Protein: 21g, Fats: 8g, Fiber: 3g, Sugar: 2g.

Recipe 4: Zesty Lime Beef Fandango

P.T.: 20 minutes
Ingr.: 200g beef chunks, lime zest, 2 tsp avocado oil, chili threads.
Serves: 2
M. of C.: Grilled

Process: Marinate beef with lime and chili. Grill. Drizzle with avocado oil.
N.V.: Carbs: 1g, Protein: 24g, Fats: 12g, Fiber: 0.5g, Sugar: 0g.

Recipe 5: Beef Stew Elysium

P.T.: 45 minutes
Ingr.: 300g lean beef cubes, carrots, celery echoes, bay leaf hint.
Serves: 4
M. of C.: Slow-cooked

Process: Combine ingredients in pot. Simmer. Serve when beef is tender.
N.V.: Carbs: 10g, Protein: 25g, Fats: 10g, Fiber: 2g, Sugar: 4g.

Recipe 6: Garlic Pepper Beef Reverie

P.T.: 25 minutes
Ingr.: 250g beef strips, garlic essence, cracked pepper song, olive oil drizzle.
Serves: 3
M. of C.: Pan-glazed

Process: Sauté beef with garlic. Season with pepper. Relish.
N.V.: Carbs: 2g, Protein: 27g, Fats: 11g, Fiber: 0.5g, Sugar: 0g.

Recipe 7: Beef Spinach Roulade

P.T.: 35 minutes
Ingr.: 150g beef slices, spinach tapestry, feta morsels, oregano whispers.
Serves: 2
M. of C.: Oven-baked

Process: Lay beef, layer with spinach and feta. Roll. Bake. Slice and serve.
N.V.: Carbs: 2g, Protein: 20g, Fats: 12g, Fiber: 1g, Sugar: 1g.

Recipe 8: Nutty Beef Broth Illusion

P.T.: 40 minutes
Ingr.: 250g beef bones, almond shreds, celery, salt trace.
Serves: 4
M. of C.: Simmered

Process: Boil beef bones. Add almond and celery. Simmer. Season. Pour.
N.V.: Carbs: 5g, Protein: 18g, Fats: 11g, Fiber: 1.5g, Sugar: 2g.

Recipe 9: Lemon Herb Beef Minuet

P.T.: 30 minutes
Ingr.: 250g beef medallions, lemon zests, rosemary, olive oil harmony.
Serves: 3
M. of C.: Pan-charred

Process: Season beef with lemon and rosemary. Sear in olive oil. Relish.
N.V.: Carbs: 0g, Protein: 29g, Fats: 13g, Fiber: 0g, Sugar: 0g.

Recipe 10: Mushroom Beef Harmony

P.T.: 35 minutes
Ingr.: 200g beef tenderloin, mushroom ensemble, thyme hint, butter waltz.
Serves: 2
M. of C.: Pan-fused

Process: Sear beef. Add mushrooms and thyme. Finish with butter. Savor.
N.V.: Carbs: 4g, Protein: 26g, Fats: 14g, Fiber: 1.5g, Sugar: 2g

Recipe 11: Tarragon Temptation Beef

P.T.: 22 minutes
Ingr.: 230g beef loin, tarragon murmur, garlic silhouette, olive oil drizzle.
Serves: 2
M. of C.: Grilled

Process: Rub beef with tarragon and garlic. Grill till tender. Plate with pan drippings.
N.V.: Carbs: 0g, Protein: 30g, Fats: 11g, Fiber: 0g, Sugar: 0g.

Recipe 12: Beefy Bean Ballad

P.T.: 40 minutes
Ingr.: 250g beef ground, black bean fragments, cumin notes, red pepper rift.
Serves: 4
M. of C.: Skillet-browned

Process: Brown beef. Stir in beans and spices. Cook until flavors meld.
N.V.: Carbs: 12g, Protein: 28g, Fats: 12g, Fiber: 5g, Sugar: 1g.

Recipe 13: Red Wine Rhapsody Beef

P.T.: 50 minutes
Ingr.: 300g beef shank, red wine reduction, onion wisps, thyme tendrils.
Serves: 3
M. of C.: Slow-braised

Process: Sear beef. Add wine, onion, and thyme. Braise until melt-in-mouth.
N.V.: Carbs: 5g, Protein: 33g, Fats: 13g, Fiber: 0.5g, Sugar: 2g.

Recipe 14: Mint Mirage Beef Skewers

P.T.: 30 minutes
Ingr.: 200g beef chunks, mint effusion, chili chimera, lemon drops.
Serves: 4
M. of C.: Char-grilled

Process: Skewer beef. Season with mint, chili, and lemon. Grill. Enjoy with dip.
N.V.: Carbs: 1g, Protein: 25g, Fats: 9g, Fiber: 0.5g, Sugar: 0g.

Recipe 15: Creamy Coconut Beef Vista

P.T.: 35 minutes
Ingr.: 250g beef slivers, coconut cream dream, turmeric touch, lemongrass lilt.
Serves: 2
M. of C.: Simmered

Process: Simmer beef in coconut cream with spices. Relish with greens.
N.V.: Carbs: 8g, Protein: 29g, Fats: 16g, Fiber: 2g, Sugar: 3g.

Recipe 16: Balsamic Beef Bravura

P.T.: 25 minutes
Ingr.: 220g beef fillet, balsamic vignette, rosemary echo, olive embrace.
Serves: 2
M. of C.: Pan-seared

Process: Sear beef. Deglaze with balsamic. Sprinkle rosemary. Plate up.
N.V.: Carbs: 5g, Protein: 31g, Fats: 12g, Fiber: 0g, Sugar: 4g.

Recipe 17: Ginger Glint Beef

P.T.: 28 minutes
Ingr.: 230g beef strips, ginger glisten, soy shadow, sesame hint.
Serves: 2
M. of C.: Wok-fried

Process: Fry beef in ginger. Splash soy. Finish with sesame. Relish hot.
N.V.: Carbs: 6g, Protein: 28g, Fats: 11g, Fiber: 1g, Sugar: 2g.

Recipe 18: Beef & Quinoa Quest

P.T.: 40 minutes
Ingr.: 240g beef morsels, quinoa choir, bell pepper burst, lime levity.
Serves: 3
M. of C.: Pan-combined

Process: Cook quinoa. Sauté beef. Mix with bell peppers and lime. Combine.
N.V.: Carbs: 23g, Protein: 29g, Fats: 10g, Fiber: 3g, Sugar: 2g.

Recipe 19: Paprika Play Beef

P.T.: 20 minutes
Ingr.: 200g beef mince, paprika pulse, tomato trail, garlic gush.
Serves: 3
M. of C.: Skillet-formed

Process: Cook beef. Stir in paprika, tomato, and garlic. Serve atop greens.
N.V.: Carbs: 8g, Protein: 26g, Fats: 11g, Fiber: 2g, Sugar: 4g.

Recipe 20: Cilantro Confluence Beef Salad

P.T.: 15 minutes
Ingr.: 180g beef tender, cilantro cascade, lemon zest, olive oil undertone.
Serves: 2
M. of C.: Thinly-sliced

Process: Grill beef. Slice. Toss in cilantro and lemon. Drizzle oil. Feast.
N.V.: Carbs: 0g, Protein: 28g, Fats: 10g, Fiber: 0g, Sugar: 0g.

Pork

Recipe 1: Lemon Lustre Pork Chops

P.T.: 18 minutes
Ingr.: 240g pork chops, lemon zephyr, garlic whisper, thyme hint.
Serves: 2
M. of C.: Grilled

Process: Marinate chops in lemon, garlic, and thyme. Grill to perfection.
N.V.: Carbs: 3g, Protein: 25g, Fats: 13g, Fiber: 0.5g, Sugar: 1g.

Recipe 2: Ginger Gaze Pork Tenderloin

P.T.: 30 minutes
Ingr.: 280g pork tenderloin, ginger radiance, soy shimmer, chili tickle.
Serves: 3
M. of C.: Roasted

Process: Rub pork with ginger, splash soy, and roast. Drizzle chili.
N.V.: Carbs: 4g, Protein: 29g, Fats: 11g, Fiber: 0.6g, Sugar: 2g.

Recipe 3: Paprika Pork Poetry

P.T.: 22 minutes
Ingr.: 220g pork ribs, paprika puff, onion murmur, vinegar veil.
Serves: 2

M. of C.: Slow-cooked
Process: Simmer ribs with paprika, onion, and vinegar. Savor soft meat.

N.V.: Carbs: 7g, Protein: 23g, Fats: 14g, Fiber: 1g, Sugar: 3g.

Recipe 4: Pork & Green Bean Gala

P.T.: 25 minutes
Ingr.: 200g pork slivers, green bean song, almond allure, lime levity.
Serves: 2
M. of C.: Pan-fried

Process: Sauté pork. Add beans, almonds, finish with lime zest. Enjoy.
N.V.: Carbs: 10g, Protein: 24g, Fats: 12g, Fiber: 3g, Sugar: 2g.

Recipe 5: Mustard Mystique Pork Roast

P.T.: 45 minutes
Ingr.: 300g pork loin, mustard musings, rosemary relic, black pepper brush.
Serves: 4
M. of C.: Oven-baked
Process: Coat pork in mustard, rosemary, and pepper. Roast to tenderness.
N.V.: Carbs: 2g, Protein: 28g, Fats: 14g, Fiber: 0.5g, Sugar: 0g.

Recipe 6: Cumin Cloud Pork Kebabs

P.T.: 20 minutes
Ingr.: 220g pork cubes, cumin canopy, yogurt yonder, cilantro curtain.
Serves: 3
M. of C.: Char-grilled

Process: Marinate pork in yogurt, cumin, and cilantro. Grill on skewers.
N.V.: Carbs: 5g, Protein: 27g, Fats: 12g, Fiber: 0.6g, Sugar: 3g.

Recipe 7: Apple Arcane Pork Salad

P.T.: 15 minutes
Ingr.: 180g pork strips, apple echo, spinach spirit, walnut wink.
Serves: 2
M. of C.: Freshly mixed

Process: Toss pork, apple, spinach, and walnuts. Drizzle light dressing.
N.V.: Carbs: 8g, Protein: 22g, Fats: 10g, Fiber: 2g, Sugar: 5g.

Recipe 8: Teriyaki Tranquil Pork

P.T.: 28 minutes
Ingr.: 240g pork belly, teriyaki twilight, sesame solace, scallion sigh.
Serves: 2
M. of C.: Pan-glazed

Process: Sear pork. Glaze with teriyaki. Sprinkle sesame and scallion.
N.V.: Carbs: 9g, Protein: 25g, Fats: 16g, Fiber: 1g, Sugar: 6g.

Recipe 9: Chili Charade Pork Bites

P.T.: 20 minutes
Ingr.: 200g pork chunks, chili cameo, lime lace, coriander chime.
Serves: 2
M. of C.: Skillet-seared

Process: Brown pork. Jazz with chili, lime, and coriander. Relish.
N.V.: Carbs: 4g, Protein: 23g, Fats: 12g, Fiber: 0.8g, Sugar: 2g.

Recipe 10: Balsamic Ballet Pork

P.T.: 30 minutes
Ingr.: 260g pork medallions, balsamic breeze, garlic glisten, thyme thrill.
Serves: 3
M. of C.: Reduction

Process: Sear pork. Deglaze with balsamic, garlic, and thyme. Revel.
N.V.: Carbs: 6g, Protein: 26g, Fats: 13g, Fiber: 0.7g, Sugar: 4g.

Recipe 11: Olive Oasis Pork Steak

P.T.: 25 minutes
Ingr.: 250g pork steak, olive omen, rosemary ripple, lemon lilt.
Serves: 2
M. of C.: Grilled

Process: Bath steak in olive, rosemary, and lemon. Grill till golden.
N.V.: Carbs: 3g, Protein: 27g, Fats: 15g, Fiber: 0.6g, Sugar: 1g.

Recipe 12: Herb Horizon Pork Skewers

P.T.: 30 minutes
Ingr.: 230g pork cubes, herb halo, pepper prism, tomato twinkle.
Serves: 3
M. of C.: Char-grilled

Process: Thread pork, seasoned with herbs and pepper, with tomatoes on skewers. Grill delightfully.
N.V.: Carbs: 5g, Protein: 26g, Fats: 13g, Fiber: 1g, Sugar: 3g.

Recipe 13: Coffee Crescendo Pork Ribs

P.T.: 45 minutes
Ingr.: 270g pork ribs, coffee caress, cocoa clue, maple murmur.
Serves: 2
M. of C.: Oven-roasted

Process: Rub ribs with coffee-cocoa mix. Drizzle with maple. Roast till tender.
N.V.: Carbs: 9g, Protein: 24g, Fats: 14g, Fiber: 0.8g, Sugar: 6g.

Recipe 14: Fennel Fantasia Pork Stew

P.T.: 50 minutes
Ingr.: 300g pork bits, fennel fantasy, carrot caress, broth balm.
Serves: 4
M. of C.: Slow-cooked

Process: Simmer pork with fennel, carrots, in a rich broth until flavors meld.
N.V.: Carbs: 8g, Protein: 28g, Fats: 12g, Fiber: 2g, Sugar: 3g.

Recipe 15: Sage Serenade Pork Sandwiches

P.T.: 20 minutes
Ingr.: 220g pork slices, sage song, whole grain whimsy, mustard muse.
Serves: 2
M. of C.: Assembled

Process: Layer pork on whole grain, infused with sage and mustard. Relish the crunch.
N.V.: Carbs: 20g, Protein: 23g, Fats: 9g, Fiber: 3g, Sugar: 2g.

Recipe 16: Peppered Pulse Pork Roll-ups

P.T.: 30 minutes
Ingr.: 240g thin pork slices, pepper palette, spinach sparkle, cheese chirp.
Serves: 2
M. of C.: Oven-baked

Process: Roll pork around spinach and cheese, seasoned with pepper. Bake till melty.
N.V.: Carbs: 2g, Protein: 28g, Fats: 14g, Fiber: 1g, Sugar: 1g.

Recipe 17: Basil Bliss Pork Sauté

P.T.: 22 minutes
Ingr.: 230g pork bits, basil burst, garlic glint, tomato trace.
Serves: 2
M. of C.: Pan-sautéed

Process: Sauté pork with basil, garlic, and tomatoes till flavors bloom.
N.V.: Carbs: 7g, Protein: 25g, Fats: 12g, Fiber: 2g, Sugar: 4g.

Recipe 18: Orange Ovation Pork Wraps

P.T.: 25 minutes

Ingr.: 210g pork shreds, orange overture, lettuce lullaby, almond aria.

Serves: 2
M. of C.: Freshly wrapped
Process: Nestle pork with orange hint in lettuce, sprinkle almonds. Enjoy the crisp.

N.V.: Carbs: 6g, Protein: 23g, Fats: 11g, Fiber: 2g, Sugar: 4g.

Recipe 19: Red Wine Rhapsody Pork

P.T.: 40 minutes
Ingr.: 280g pork medallions, red wine riddle, onion opera, herb hymn.
Serves: 3
M. of C.: Simmered

Process: Sear pork. Simmer in wine, onions, and herbs till harmony.
N.V.: Carbs: 9g, Protein: 29g, Fats: 13g, Fiber: 1g, Sugar: 4g.

Recipe 20: Vanilla Vapor Pork Curry

P.T.: 45 minutes
Ingr.: 300g pork cubes, vanilla veil, coconut chorus, spice symphony.
Serves: 4
M. of C.: Slow-cooked

Process: Cook pork in coconut milk, infused with vanilla and spices. Savor the melody.
N.V.: Carbs: 7g, Protein: 27g, Fats: 15g, Fiber: 1.5g, Sugar: 3g.

Lamb

Recipe 1: Lavender Lure Lamb Chops

P.T.: 30 minutes
Ingr.: 250g lamb chops, lavender limelight, rosemary ripple, olive opus.
Serves: 2
M. of C.: Grilled

Process: Marinate chops in lavender, rosemary, and olive blend. Grill to perfection.
N.V.: Carbs: 2g, Protein: 29g, Fats: 17g, Fiber: 0.5g, Sugar: 1g.

Recipe 2: Minty Mirage Lamb Stew

P.T.: 50 minutes
Ingr.: 280g lamb cubes, mint matrix, potato puzzle, broth ballad.
Serves: 3
M. of C.: Slow-cooked

Process: Simmer lamb with potatoes in a mint-infused broth. Relish the warm embrace.
N.V.: Carbs: 18g, Protein: 30g, Fats: 14g, Fiber: 2.5g, Sugar: 3g.

Recipe 3: Terra Tang Lamb Wraps

P.T.: 20 minutes
Ingr.: 230g spiced lamb shreds, lettuce lyric, cucumber chorus, yogurt yodel.
Serves: 2
M. of C.: Freshly wrapped

Process: Cradle lamb in lettuce, garnished with cucumber. Drizzle yogurt. Enjoy.
N.V.: Carbs: 8g, Protein: 28g, Fats: 13g, Fiber: 1g, Sugar: 4g.

Recipe 4: Berry Bliss Lamb Skewers

P.T.: 35 minutes
Ingr.: 240g lamb pieces, berry burst, thyme thread, pepper prism.
Serves: 3
M. of C.: Char-grilled

Process: Skewer lamb and berries, sprinkle thyme and pepper. Grill with zest.
N.V.: Carbs: 5g, Protein: 31g, Fats: 16g, Fiber: 1g, Sugar: 4g.

Recipe 5: Tarragon Twilight Lamb Steaks

P.T.: 25 minutes
Ingr.: 260g lamb steaks, tarragon tapestry, garlic glint, zucchini zest.
Serves: 2
M. of C.: Pan-seared
Process: Sear lamb seasoned with tarragon and garlic. Pair with zucchini.
N.V.: Carbs: 6g, Protein: 29g, Fats: 15g, Fiber: 1.2g, Sugar: 2g.

Recipe 6: Orange Oasis Lamb Curry

P.T.: 40 minutes
Ingr.: 270g lamb cubes, orange overture, coconut canvas, spice spectrum.
Serves: 4
M. of C.: Slow-cooked
Process: Simmer lamb in coconut and orange infusion. Spice as desired.
N.V.: Carbs: 9g, Protein: 28g, Fats: 18g, Fiber: 2g, Sugar: 5g.

Recipe 7: Ginger Gleam Lamb Soup

P.T.: 35 minutes
Ingr.: 250g minced lamb, ginger glow, spinach sparkle, broth ballad.

Serves: 3
M. of C.: Simmered

Process: Blend lamb with ginger in spinach broth. Comfort in every sip.

N.V.: Carbs: 7g, Protein: 27g, Fats: 12g, Fiber: 1.5g, Sugar: 2g.

Recipe 8: Anise Arch Lamb Roast

P.T.: 1 hour
Ingr.: 300g lamb roast, anise anthem, carrot caress, celery cipher.
Serves: 4
M. of C.: Oven-roasted

Process: Coat lamb in anise. Roast with carrots and celery. Relish the aroma.
N.V.: Carbs: 8g, Protein: 32g, Fats: 15g, Fiber: 2g, Sugar: 3g.

Recipe 9: Chili Charm Lamb Burgers

P.T.: 30 minutes
Ingr.: 230g minced lamb, chili chime, lettuce lullaby, tomato twinkle.
Serves: 2
M. of C.: Pan-fried

Process: Form lamb patties, infuse chili. Fry, then sandwich in lettuce with tomato.
N.V.: Carbs: 6g, Protein: 30g, Fats: 14g, Fiber: 1.2g, Sugar: 2.5g.

Recipe 10: Olive Ovation Lamb Salad

P.T.: 20 minutes
Ingr.: 200g grilled lamb slices, olive opera, feta fantasy, walnut whisper.
Serves: 2
M. of C.: Freshly tossed

Process: Toss lamb with olives, feta, and walnuts. Revel in the fusion.
N.V.: Carbs: 5g, Protein: 29g, Fats: 17g, Fiber: 1.3g, Sugar: 2g.

Recipe 11: Lemony Lull Lamb Ribs

P.T.: 45 minutes
Ingr.: 270g lamb ribs, lemony liaison, thyme tether, olive obelisk.
Serves: 3
M. of C.: Oven-roasted

Process: Massage ribs with lemon and thyme. Roast with a splash of olive elixir.
N.V.: Carbs: 3g, Protein: 33g, Fats: 20g, Fiber: 0.8g, Sugar: 1g.

Recipe 12: Basil Bliss Lamb Kebabs

P.T.: 35 minutes
Ingr.: 230g lamb cubes, basil buoyancy, yogurt yonder, bell pepper ballet.
Serves: 2
M. of C.: Char-grilled

Process: Skewer lamb and peppers. Brush with basil-yogurt harmony. Grill.
N.V.: Carbs: 5g, Protein: 28g, Fats: 16g, Fiber: 1.4g, Sugar: 3g.

Recipe 13: Rhubarb Radiance Lamb Tacos

P.T.: 30 minutes
Ingr.: 250g spiced lamb shreds, rhubarb rhapsody, avocado aria, lettuce lithograph.
Serves: 2
M. of C.: Freshly wrapped

Process: Enclose lamb and rhubarb in a lettuce sheet. Crown with avocado.
N.V.: Carbs: 9g, Protein: 30g, Fats: 15g, Fiber: 2.8g, Sugar: 4g.

Recipe 14: Apricot Arc Lamb Stir-fry

P.T.: 25 minutes
Ingr.: 240g lamb slices, apricot anthem, ginger glyphs, broccoli balladeer.
Serves: 3
M. of C.: Stir-fried

Process: Wok-sauté lamb with apricot and ginger. Integrate broccoli brilliance.
N.V.: Carbs: 12g, Protein: 29g, Fats: 14g, Fiber: 3g, Sugar: 5g.

Recipe 15: Fennel Fable Lamb Casserole

P.T.: 1 hour
Ingr.: 280g lamb chunks, fennel folklore, tomato tome, oregano ode.
Serves: 4
M. of C.: Slow-cooked

Process: Nestle lamb in fennel and tomato concoction. Slow-cook with oregano essence.
N.V.: Carbs: 9g, Protein: 31g, Fats: 17g, Fiber: 2.5g, Sugar: 4g.

Recipe 16: Pecan Pageantry Lamb Bites

P.T.: 25 minutes
Ingr.: 220g minced lamb, pecan panorama, rosemary rendering, cheese chant.
Serves: 2
M. of C.: Baked

Process: Intermingle lamb with pecans and rosemary. Bake. Garnish with cheese charms.
N.V.: Carbs: 6g, Protein: 28g, Fats: 19g, Fiber: 1.7g, Sugar: 2g.

Recipe 17: Saffron Symphony Lamb Curry

P.T.: 50 minutes
Ingr.: 300g lamb cubes, saffron serenade, coconut cadence, chili chanson.
Serves: 4
M. of C.: Slow-cooked

Process: Unveil lamb in saffron-coconut melody. Spice with chili undertones.
N.V.: Carbs: 8g, Protein: 32g, Fats: 18g, Fiber: 2g, Sugar: 3g.

Recipe 18: Mushroom Mural Lamb Pie

P.T.: 1 hour 15 minutes
Ingr.: 280g minced lamb, mushroom mosaic, thyme tableau, almond artistry (for crust).
Serves: 4

M. of C.: Baked
Process: Unite lamb with mushrooms and thyme. Envelop in almond artistry. Bake.
N.V.: Carbs: 10g, Protein: 30g, Fats: 16g, Fiber: 2.8g, Sugar: 2g.

Recipe 19: Pear Parable Lamb Salad

P.T.: 20 minutes
Ingr.: 200g grilled lamb strips, pear parabola, spinach sonnet, walnut wisdom.
Serves: 2
M. of C.: Freshly tossed

Process: Toss lamb with pear and spinach. Top with walnut wonders.
N.V.: Carbs: 12g, Protein: 28g, Fats: 15g, Fiber: 2g, Sugar: 5g.

Recipe 20: Cumin Canvas Lamb Skewers

P.T.: 40 minutes
Ingr.: 230g lamb cubes, cumin constellation, garlic gazette, olive oracle.
Serves: 2
M. of C.: Char-grilled

Process: Infuse lamb with cumin and garlic grandeur. Skewer. Char-grill.
N.V.: Carbs: 5g, Protein: 29g, Fats: 16g, Fiber: 1.2g, Sugar: 1g.

Chicken

Recipe 1: Tarragon Tapestry Chicken Thighs

P.T.: 35 minutes
Ingr.: 300g chicken thighs, tarragon testament, lemon lore, olive offering.
Serves: 3
M. of C.: Oven-baked

Process: Lavish thighs with tarragon, lemon zest, and olive emblem. Oven-bake.
N.V.: Carbs: 4g, Protein: 28g, Fats: 16g, Fiber: 1g, Sugar: 1g

Recipe 2: Cilantro Cynosure Chicken Salad

P.T.: 20 minutes
Ingr.: 220g grilled chicken breast, cilantro crown, avocado anthem, cherry tomato tale.
Serves: 2

M. of C.: Freshly tossed
Process: Intertwine chicken with cilantro, avocado, and tomatoes. Serve cool.

N.V.: Carbs: 6g, Protein: 30g, Fats: 14g, Fiber: 3g, Sugar: 3g.

Recipe 3: Garlic Galaxy Chicken Soup

P.T.: 50 minutes
Ingr.: 250g chicken shreds, garlic globe, spinach saga, almond allure.
Serves: 4
M. of C.: Simmered

Process: Brew chicken in garlic effulgence. Add spinach and almond accents.
N.V.: Carbs: 7g, Protein: 26g, Fats: 11g, Fiber: 2.4g, Sugar: 1.5g.

Recipe 4: Sage Symphony Chicken Wraps

P.T.: 30 minutes
Ingr.: 230g spiced chicken, sage sonnet, lettuce lexicon, mustard mural.
Serves: 3
M. of C.: Freshly wrapped

Process: Envelop chicken and sage in lettuce. Drizzle with mustard memento.
N.V.: Carbs: 5g, Protein: 28g, Fats: 14g, Fiber: 1.8g, Sugar: 2g.

Recipe 5: Basil Ballet Chicken Kebabs

Ingr.: 260g chicken cubes, basil ballad, yogurt yarn, bell pepper panorama.
Serves: 3
M. of C.: Char-grilled
Process: Skewer chicken, bathe in basil-yogurt blend. Grill with bell pepper pieces.
N.V.: Carbs: 6g, Protein: 30g, Fats: 15g, Fiber: 2g, Sugar: 3g.

P.T.: 40 minutes

Recipe 6: Chive Charade Chicken Stir-fry

P.T.: 25 minutes
Ingr.: 240g chicken slices, chive chorus, ginger glyph, snap pea spectacle.
Serves: 3
M. of C.: Stir-fried

Process: Sauté chicken with chive and ginger garnish. Integrate snap pea spark.
N.V.: Carbs: 8g, Protein: 29g, Fats: 12g, Fiber: 3g, Sugar: 4g.

Recipe 7: Oregano Odyssey Chicken Pie

P.T.: 1 hour 10 minutes

Ingr.: 280g minced chicken, oregano oracle, mushroom memoir, almond artistry (for crust).
Serves: 4
M. of C.: Baked

Process: Unite chicken with mushroom and oregano opulence. Enshroud in almond armor. Bake.
N.V.: Carbs: 9g, Protein: 31g, Fats: 15g, Fiber: 3g, Sugar: 2g.

Recipe 8: Thyme Theater Chicken Casserole

P.T.: 55 minutes
Ingr.: 300g chicken chunks, thyme tableau, coconut cadenza, chili chapbook.
Serves: 4
M. of C.: Slow-cooked

Process: Enthrall chicken in thyme-coconut tune. Spice with chili charisma.
N.V.: Carbs: 7g, Protein: 30g, Fats: 14g, Fiber: 2.5g, Sugar: 3g.

Recipe 9: Lemon Lilt Chicken Soup

P.T.: 50 minutes
Ingr.: 260g chicken morsels, lemon lore, celery cinema, parsley parable.
Serves: 4
M. of C.: Simmered

Process: Engulf chicken in lemon-laced broth. Accent with celery and parsley.
N.V.: Carbs: 8g, Protein: 28g, Fats: 11g, Fiber: 2g, Sugar: 3g.

Recipe 10: Mint Motif Chicken Tacos

P.T.: 35 minutes
Ingr.: 250g spiced chicken shreds, mint mosaic, avocado aria, almond armor (for crust).
Serves: 3

M. of C.: Freshly compiled
Process: Engage chicken and mint in an almond embrace. Adorn with avocado.
N.V.: Carbs: 10g, Protein: 30g, Fats: 16g, Fiber: 4g, Sugar: 2g.

Recipe 11: Parsley Pageant Chicken Roulade

P.T.: 50 minutes
Ingr.: 300g chicken breasts, parsley panorama, feta filament, olive oracle.
Serves: 3
M. of C.: Oven-baked

Process: Layer chicken with feta and parsley parable. Roll, secure, and bake in olive ode.
N.V.: Carbs: 2g, Protein: 32g, Fats: 13g, Fiber: 1g, Sugar: 1g.

Recipe 12: Coriander Coronation Chicken Patties

P.T.: 40 minutes

Ingr.: 280g minced chicken, coriander crown, flaxseed fable, coconut charm.

Serves: 4
M. of C.: Pan-fried
Process: Intertwine minced chicken with coriander, shape with flaxseed, and pan-fry in coconut charisma.

N.V.: Carbs: 5g, Protein: 31g, Fats: 14g, Fiber: 3g, Sugar: 1g.

Recipe 13: Dill Delight Chicken Broth

P.T.: 1 hour
Ingr.: 320g chicken bones, dill diary, celery cinema, ginger glyph.
Serves: 4
M. of C.: Slow-simmered

Process: Distill chicken bones in a pot. Imbue with dill, celery, and ginger gleams.
N.V.: Carbs: 6g, Protein: 28g, Fats: 10g, Fiber: 2g, Sugar: 2g.

Recipe 14: Marjoram Muse Chicken Quiche

P.T.: 1 hour 15 minutes
Ingr.: 250g diced chicken, marjoram memoir, almond armor, mushroom mystery.
Serves: 4
M. of C.: Oven-baked

Process: Enfold chicken, marjoram, and mushrooms within almond armor. Oven bake.
N.V.: Carbs: 8g, Protein: 30g, Fats: 16g, Fiber: 3g, Sugar: 2g.

Recipe 15: Fenugreek Fantasy Chicken Curry

P.T.: 45 minutes
Ingr.: 300g chicken chunks, fenugreek fable, coconut cadence, turmeric tome.
Serves: 4
M. of C.: Slow-cooked

Process: Immerse chicken in fenugreek festivity and coconut choir. Color with turmeric tint.
N.V.: Carbs: 7g, Protein: 31g, Fats: 14g, Fiber: 2g, Sugar: 3g.

Recipe 16: Lavender Lullaby Chicken Salad

P.T.: 25 minutes
Ingr.: 220g roasted chicken, lavender lexicon, arugula anthem, walnut whisper.
Serves: 3
M. of C.: Freshly tossed

Process: Layer chicken with arugula and lavender lilt. Top with walnut wonders.
N.V.: Carbs: 5g, Protein: 29g, Fats: 15g, Fiber: 2.5g, Sugar: 2g.

Recipe 17: Anise Aria Chicken Stew

P.T.: 1 hour

Ingr.: 320g chicken shreds, anise anthem, tomato tableau, olive oracle.

Serves: 4
M. of C.: Slow-cooked
Process: Baptize chicken in anise allure, blend with tomato and olive odyssey.

N.V.: Carbs: 10g, Protein: 30g, Fats: 14g, Fiber: 3g, Sugar: 4g.

Recipe 18: Bay Leaf Ballet Chicken Roast

P.T.: 1 hour 20 minutes
Ingr.: 400g chicken, bay leaf ballad, lemon lore, garlic galaxy.
Serves: 4
M. of C.: Oven-roasted

Process: Adorn chicken with bay leaf, lemon, and garlic glimmers. Roast regally.
N.V.: Carbs: 6g, Protein: 32g, Fats: 15g, Fiber: 2g, Sugar: 2g.

Recipe 19: Juniper Jive Chicken Skewers

P.T.: 40 minutes
Ingr.: 260g chicken tenders, juniper jazz, bell pepper panorama, onion opera.
Serves: 3
M. of C.: Char-grilled

Process: Skewer chicken, alternating with juniper jewels, pepper, and onion odes.
N.V.: Carbs: 7g, Protein: 29g, Fats: 12g, Fiber: 2.5g, Sugar: 3g.

Recipe 20: Chicory Chorus Chicken Zoodles

P.T.: 30 minutes
Ingr.: 240g grilled chicken, chicory chant, zucchini zodiac, almond allure.
Serves: 3
M. of C.: Lightly sautéed

Process: Sauté chicken in chicory cadence. Intertwine with zucchini zephyrs.
N.V.: Carbs: 8g, Protein:28g, Fats: 13g, Fiber: 3g, Sugar: 3g.

Fish and Seafood

Recipe 1: Basil Brine Baked Salmon

P.T.: 35 minutes
Ingr.: 220g salmon fillet, basil boon, lemon limelight, olive oracle.
Serves: 2
M. of C.: Oven-baked

Process: Lavish salmon with basil bouquet, and lemon lyric. Bake in olive odyssey.
N.V.: Carbs: 2g, Protein: 34g, Fats: 15g, Fiber: 1g, Sugar: 1g.

Recipe 2: Tarragon Tide Tuna Tartare

P.T.: 20 minutes
Ingr.: 200g raw tuna, tarragon trance, avocado anthem, sesame symphony.
Serves: 2
M. of C.: Freshly prepared

Process: Merge tuna with tarragon, avocado aria, and sesame serenade.
N.V.: Carbs: 5g, Protein: 32g, Fats: 14g, Fiber: 3g, Sugar: 1g.

Recipe 3: Dill Drizzle Cod Ceviche

P.T.: 40 minutes
Ingr.: 230g cod cubes, dill drench, lime luminary, chili chorus.
Serves: 3
M. of C.: Chilled marinated

Process: Infuse cod with dill, lime legend, and chili chime. Chill.
N.V.: Carbs: 4g, Protein: 31g, Fats: 13g, Fiber: 2g, Sugar: 2g.

Recipe 4: Saffron Stream Shrimp Stir-fry

P.T.: 25 minutes
Ingr.: 250g shrimps, saffron story, bell pepper ballad, ginger glyph.
Serves: 3
M. of C.: Pan-sautéed

Process: Sauté shrimps in saffron saga with bell pepper and ginger gleams.
N.V.: Carbs: 6g, Protein: 29g, Fats: 12g, Fiber: 2.5g, Sugar: 2g.

Recipe 5: Coriander Cove Crab Salad

P.T.: 15 minutes
Ingr.: 220g crab meat, coriander chronicle, cucumber charisma, almond allure.
Serves: 2
M. of C.: Freshly tossed

Process: Intertwine crab with coriander, cucumber charm, and almond aria.
N.V.: Carbs: 5g, Protein: 28g, Fats: 13g, Fiber: 3g, Sugar: 2g.

Recipe 6: Mint Mirage Mackerel Grill

P.T.: 40 minutes

Ingr.: 240g mackerel, mint memoir, lemon limelight, garlic galaxy.
Serves: 2
M. of C.: Char-grilled
Process: Graced mackerel with mint melody, lemon, and garlic glimmers. Grill gracefully.
N.V.: Carbs: 3g, Protein: 32g, Fats: 14g, Fiber: 1g, Sugar: 1g.

Recipe 7: Fennel Fantasy Flounder Fry

P.T.: 30 minutes
Ingr.: 230g flounder fillet, fennel fable, coconut cadence, turmeric tome.
Serves: 3
M. of C.: Lightly fried

Process: Adorn flounder with fennel festivity and coconut choir. Fry with turmeric tint.
N.V.: Carbs: 6g, Protein: 30g, Fats: 15g, Fiber: 2g, Sugar: 2g.

Recipe 8: Thyme Tide Tilapia Tacos

P.T.: 40 minutes
Ingr.: 240g grilled tilapia, thyme theme, avocado anthem, lettuce lexicon.
Serves: 3
M. of C.: Grilled & assembled

Process: Place tilapia tinted with thyme within a lettuce lore, crowned with avocado aria.
N.V.: Carbs: 7g, Protein: 28g, Fats: 14g, Fiber: 3g, Sugar: 3g.

Recipe 9: Oregano Ocean Octopus Stir-fry

P.T.: 45 minutes
Ingr.: 250g octopus chunks, oregano ode, tomato tableau, olive oracle.
Serves: 3
M. of C.: Pan-sautéed

Process: Sauté octopus in olive odyssey, blend with oregano and tomato tones.
N.V.: Carbs: 8g, Protein: 29g, Fats: 13g, Fiber: 2.5g, Sugar: 3g.

Recipe 10: Rosemary Ripple Red Snapper

P.T.: 40 minutes
Ingr.: 260
g red snapper, rosemary rhyme, lemon limelight, caper chorus.
Serves: 3
M. of C.: Oven-baked

Process: Embellish snapper with rosemary reverie, lemon and caper chords. Bake to brilliance.
N.V.: Carbs: 3g, Protein: 33g, Fats: 14g, Fiber: 1.5g, Sugar: 2g.

Recipe 11: Chive Charade Clam Chowder

P.T.: 50 minutes
Ingr.: 300g fresh clams, chive chronicle, celery cinema, almond allure broth.
Serves: 4
M. of C.: Slow-cooked

Process: Simmer clams in almond aria, season with chive charisma, and introduce celery cine-films.
N.V.: Carbs: 9g, Protein: 18g, Fats: 12g, Fiber: 3g, Sugar: 3g.

Recipe 12: Parsley Promenade Prawn Pilaf

P.T.: 45 minutes
Ingr.: 320g prawns, parsley parade, cauliflower cinema, lemon limelight.
Serves: 4
M. of C.: Pan-seared & steamed

Process: Sequester prawns with parsley panorama and lemon. Steam atop cauliflower cinema.
N.V.: Carbs: 8g, Protein: 20g, Fats: 11g, Fiber: 4g, Sugar: 2g.

Recipe 13: Ginger Gusto Grilled Grouper

P.T.: 40 minutes
Ingr.: 270g grouper fillet, ginger glyph, lime luminary, thyme theme.
Serves: 3
M. of C.: Char-grilled

Process: Gift grouper with ginger gleams, lime lullaby, and thyme tones. Grill grandly.
N.V.: Carbs: 7g, Protein: 31g, Fats: 14g, Fiber: 2g, Sugar: 2g.

Recipe 14: Lavender Lure Lobster Linguine

P.T.: 60 minutes
Ingr.: 240g lobster meat, lavender lexicon, zucchini zephyr linguine, almond allure.
Serves: 3
M. of C.: Sauteed & simmered

Process: Luxuriate lobster in lavender litany, lay atop zucchini zest linguine and almond accents.
N.V.: Carbs: 10g, Protein: 29g, Fats: 15g, Fiber: 4g, Sugar: 3g.

Recipe 15: Sage Symphony Scallop Skewers

P.T.: 35 minutes
Ingr.: 220g scallops, sage soliloquy, lemon limelight, garlic galaxy.
Serves: 2
M. of C.: Char-grilled

Process: Serenade scallops with sage, lemon lyrics, and garlic glistens. Grill gallantly.
N.V.: Carbs: 5g, Protein: 28g, Fats: 12g, Fiber: 2g, Sugar: 2g.

Recipe 16: Anise Aria Anchovy Avocado Toast

P.T.: 15 minutes
Ingr.: 150g anchovies, anise anthem, avocado arcadia, flaxseed folklore bread.
Serves: 2
M. of C.: Assembled & toasted

Process: Array anchovies atop avocado allure on flaxseed fable. Add anise accents and toast.
N.V.: Carbs: 12g, Protein: 25g, Fats: 14g, Fiber: 6g, Sugar: 1g.

Recipe 17: Cumin Concert Calamari Rings

P.T.: 25 minutes
Ingr.: 260g calamari, cumin chorus, chili chime, olive oracle.
Serves: 3
M. of C.: Lightly fried

Process: Charm calamari with cumin cadence and chili chant. Fry in olive opus lightly.
N.V.: Carbs: 9g, Protein: 24g, Fats: 13g, Fiber: 2g, Sugar: 2g.

Recipe 18: Marjoram Mirage Mussel Marinara

P.T.: 45 minutes
Ingr.: 280g mussels, marjoram memoir, tomato tableau, garlic galaxy.
Serves: 4
M. of C.: Simmered

Process: Muse mussels in marjoram milieu, meld with tomato tones and garlic gleams.
N.V.: Carbs: 8g, Protein: 19g, Fats: 12g, Fiber: 3g, Sugar: 4g.

Recipe 19: Vanilla Vignette Velvet Crab Soup

P.T.: 50 minutes
Ingr.: 220g crab meat, vanilla verse, coconut cadence, lemongrass limerick.
Serves: 4
M. of C.: Slow-cooked

Process: Vault crab in vanilla vista, complement with coconut choir and lemongrass lyric.
N.V.: Carbs: 11g, Protein: 17g, Fats: 14g, Fiber: 2g, Sugar: 4g.

Recipe 20: Fennel Fantasy Fish Fritters

P.T.: 30 minutes
Ingr.: 290g mixed fish fillet, fennel fable, almond allure, chive chronicle.
Serves: 4
M. of C.: Pan-fried

Process: Fashion fish with fennel fiction and chive charisma. Fry in almond ambience.
N.V.: Carbs: 9g, Protein: 26g, Fats: 15g, Fiber: 3g, Sugar: 3g.

Soups

Recipe 1: Zucchini Zenith Zest

P.T.: 35 minutes
Ingr.: Zucchini zodiac, onion ode, garlic galaxy, olive oracle.

Serves: 4
M. of C.: Blended

Process: Zestfully zizzle zucchini, onion opus, and garlic gleams in olive aura. Blitz to brilliance.

N.V.: Carbs: 7g, Protein: 2g, Fats: 8g, Fiber: 2g, Sugar: 4g.

Recipe 2: Tomato Twilight Tingle

P.T.: 40 minutes
Ingr.: Tomato tableau, celery cinema, basil ballet, almond allure.
Serves: 3
M. of C.: Simmered

Process: Tantalize tomatoes with celery cine-films and basil breeze. Simmer in almond aria.
N.V.: Carbs: 9g, Protein: 3g, Fats: 6g, Fiber: 3g, Sugar: 5g.

Recipe 3: Fennel Fantasy Fusion

P.T.: 45 minutes
Ingr.: Fennel fable, leek lore, lemon limelight, coconut cadence.
Serves: 3
M. of C.: Slow-cooked

Process: Fashion fennel and leek legends in lemon luminance. Complete with coconut choir.
N.V.: Carbs: 8g, Protein: 2g, Fats: 8g, Fiber: 2g, Sugar: 3g.

Recipe 4: Mushroom Melody Mingle

P.T.: 50 minutes
Ingr.: Mushroom memoir, thyme theme, almond allure, chive chronicle.
Serves: 4
M. of C.: Blended

Process: Mingle mushroom musings with thyme tones and chive charisma. Merge with almond ambience.
N.V.: Carbs: 10g, Protein: 5g, Fats: 9g, Fiber: 3g, Sugar: 3g.

Recipe 5: Spinach Sonata Silk

P.T.: 35 minutes
Ingr.: Spinach saga, garlic galaxy, ginger glyph, lemon limelight.
Serves: 3
M. of C.: Puréed

Process: Serenade spinach in garlic gleams and ginger glimpses. Pour with a touch of lemon.
N.V.: Carbs: 6g, Protein: 2g, Fats: 7g, Fiber: 2g, Sugar: 2g.

Recipe 6: Celery Canto Cream

P.T.: 40 minutes
Ingr.: Celery cinema, onion ode, thyme theme, coconut cadence.
Serves: 4

M. of C.: Slow-cooked
Process: Caress celery and onion oratory in a thyme theater. Culminate with coconut crescendo.

N.V.: Carbs: 8g, Protein: 2g, Fats: 8g, Fiber: 3g, Sugar: 4g.

Recipe 7: Broccoli Ballad Bliss

P.T.: 30 minutes

Ingr.: Broccoli ballade, almond allure, lemon limelight, garlic galaxy.
Serves: 4
M. of C.: Blended
Process: Ballet broccoli with almond aroma. Blend with garlic gleams and lemon.
N.V.: Carbs: 9g, Protein: 4g, Fats: 8g, Fiber: 4g, Sugar: 2g.

Recipe 8: Cauliflower Cantata Charm

P.T.: 35 minutes
Ingr.: Cauliflower chorus, chive chronicle, garlic galaxy, coconut cadence.
Serves: 3
M. of C.: Puréed

Process: Choreograph cauliflower, chive, and garlic gala. Concoct with coconut canticle.
N.V.: Carbs: 8g, Protein: 3g, Fats: 9g, Fiber: 3g, Sugar: 3g.

Recipe 9: Pumpkin Prelude Potion

P.T.: 45 minutes
Ingr.: Pumpkin prose, ginger glyph, cinnamon cine-film, almond allure.
Serves: 4
M. of C.: Slow-cooked

Process: Parade pumpkin with ginger and cinnamon cinema. Pour almond aria.
N.V.: Carbs: 12g, Protein: 3g, Fats: 8g, Fiber: 3g, Sugar: 5g.

Recipe 10: Lentil Lyric Lagoon

P.T.: 60 minutes
Ingr.: Lentil lullaby, carrot charisma, onion ode, basil ballet.
Serves: 4
M. of C.: Simmered

Process: Luxuriate lentils, carrot cadences, and onion opus in basil breezes.
N.V.: Carbs: 20g, Protein: 9g, Fats: 6g, Fiber: 8g, Sugar: 4g.

Recipe 11: Beetroot Ballad Broth

P.T.: 40 minutes
Ingr.: Beetroot biography, ginger glyph, lemon limelight, celery cinema.
Serves: 3
M. of C.: Slow-cooked

Process: Brew beetroot brilliance with ginger glimpses. Cascade with celery cinematography and a lilt of lemon.
N.V.: Carbs: 11g, Protein: 3g, Fats: 1g, Fiber: 3g, Sugar: 8g.

Recipe 12: Asparagus Aria Alchemy

P.T.: 30 minutes
Ingr.: Asparagus anthology, garlic galaxy, lemon limelight, thyme theme.
Serves: 4
M. of C.: Puréed

Process: Align asparagus art with garlic gleams. Punctuate with lemon lyrics and thyme theatre.
N.V.: Carbs: 6g, Protein: 2g, Fats: 5g, Fiber: 2g, Sugar: 3g.

Recipe 13: Pepper Prelude Potion

P.T.: 45 minutes
Ingr.: Red pepper romance, onion ode, basil ballet, olive oracle.
Serves: 4
M. of C.: Blended

Process: Perform with pepper, onion oratory, and basil breezes. Perfect with an olive overture.
N.V.: Carbs: 9g, Protein: 2g, Fats: 6g, Fiber: 3g, Sugar: 5g.

Recipe 14: Cabbage Cantata Comfort

P.T.: 35 minutes
Ingr.: Cabbage canvas, carrot charisma, garlic galaxy, ginger glyph.
Serves: 3
M. of C.: Slow-cooked

Process: Celebrate cabbage and carrot choreography with garlic and ginger grace.
N.V.: Carbs: 10g, Protein: 3g, Fats: 2g, Fiber: 4g, Sugar: 5g.

Recipe 15: Green Bean Ballade Bliss

P.T.: 40 minutes
Ingr.: Green bean gallery, thyme theme, lemon limelight, almond allure.
Serves: 4
M. of C.: Simmered

Process: Gather green beans and thyme tones. Simmer with lemon lullaby and almond ambience.
N.V.: Carbs: 8g, Protein: 3g, Fats: 7g, Fiber: 3g, Sugar: 2g.

Recipe 16: Radish Rhapsody Rapture

P.T.: 30 minutes

Ingr.: Radish requiem, celery cinema, ginger glyph, coconut cadence.

Serves: 3
M. of C.: Puréed
Process: Render radish with celery cine-films and ginger grace. Rally with coconut choir.

N.V.: Carbs: 7g, Protein: 2g, Fats: 6g, Fiber: 2g, Sugar: 3g.

Recipe 17: Sweet Potato Symphony Soup

P.T.: 50 minutes
Ingr.: Sweet potato soliloquy, onion ode, ginger glyph, thyme theme.
Serves: 4
M. of C.: Slow-cooked

Process: Showcase sweet potato sonnets with onion oratory. Integrate with ginger and thyme tones.
N.V.: Carbs: 20g, Protein: 3g, Fats: 1g, Fiber: 4g, Sugar: 5g.

Recipe 18: Turnip Tune Temptation

P.T.: 40 minutes
Ingr.: Turnip tableau, garlic galaxy, celery cinema, basil ballet.
Serves: 3
M. of C.: Blended

Process: Toast turnip tales with garlic gleams and celery cinematography. Top with basil brilliance.
N.V.: Carbs: 8g, Protein: 2g, Fats: 5g, Fiber: 3g, Sugar: 3g.

Recipe 19: Parsnip Prose Pleasure

P.T.: 45 minutes
Ingr.: Parsnip poem, leek lore, cinnamon cine-film, almond allure.
Serves: 4
M. of C.: Slow-cooked

Process: Parley parsnip and leek lyrics with cinnamon cinema. Pair with almond aria.
N.V.: Carbs: 15g, Protein: 3g, Fats: 6g, Fiber: 4g, Sugar: 5g.

Recipe 20: Butternut Ballet Broth

P.T.: 50 minutes
Ingr.: Butternut ballade, onion ode, thyme theme, olive oracle.
Serves: 4
M. of C.: Simmered

Process: Blend butternut brilliance with onion oratory and thyme theatre. Bless with olive overture.
N.V.: Carbs: 12g, Protein: 2g, Fats: 8g, Fiber: 3g, Sugar: 4g.

Vegetables

Recipe 1: Zucchini Zen Zest

P.T.: 25 minutes
Ingr.: Zucchini zephyr, garlic galaxy, tomato tableau, basil ballet.
Serves: 3
M. of C.: Sautéed

Process: Sizzle zucchini zenith with garlic gleams. Tango with tomato and basil breezes.
N.V.: Carbs: 8g, Protein: 3g, Fats: 4g, Fiber: 2g, Sugar: 5g.

Recipe 2: Eggplant Elegy Embrace

P.T.: 35 minutes
Ingr.: Eggplant epic, onion ode, pepper prelude, thyme theme.
Serves: 4
M. of C.: Grilled

Process: Engage eggplant essence with onion oratory. Grace with pepper and thyme tones.
N.V.: Carbs: 12g, Protein: 3g, Fats: 5g, Fiber: 4g, Sugar: 6g.

Recipe 3: Cabbage Canvas Cantata

P.T.: 30 minutes
Ingr.: Cabbage chronicle, carrot charisma, garlic galaxy, ginger glyph.
Serves: 3
M. of C.: Steamed

Process: Champion cabbage and carrot choreography. Glimmer with garlic and ginger grace.
N.V.: Carbs: 9g, Protein: 2g, Fats: 3g, Fiber: 3g, Sugar: 4g.

Recipe 4: Brussels Brio Ballet

P.T.: 45 minutes
Ingr.: Brussels sprouts saga, bacon ballad, onion ode, pepper prelude.
Serves: 4
M. of C.: Roasted

Process: Bask Brussels with bacon beats and onion opera. Punctuate with pepper prose.
N.V.: Carbs: 11g, Protein: 6g, Fats: 8g, Fiber: 4g, Sugar: 3g.

Recipe 5: Cauliflower Cadence Carousel

P.T.: 30 minutes
Ingr.: Cauliflower canvas, almond allure, lemon limelight, thyme theme.
Serves: 3
M. of C.: Baked
Process: Celebrate cauliflower craft with almond aria. Light with lemon and thyme.
N.V.: Carbs: 9g, Protein: 4g, Fats: 7g, Fiber: 4g, Sugar: 3g.

Recipe 6: Spinach Soliloquy Symphony

P.T.: 20 minutes
Ingr.: Spinach sonnet, garlic galaxy, mushroom muse, nutmeg narrative.
Serves: 3
M. of C.: Sautéed

Process: Sauté spinach saga with garlic glimmers and mushroom melody. Nestle with nutmeg notes.
N.V.: Carbs: 6g, Protein: 4g, Fats: 5g, Fiber: 3g, Sugar: 2g.

Recipe 7: Bell Pepper Ballade Bliss

P.T.: 35 minutes
Ingr.: Bell pepper panorama, quinoa quintet, corn chorus, cilantro cadence.
Serves: 4
M. of C.: Stuffed & Baked

Process: Present peppers with quinoa quavers. Crown with corn cantata and cilantro crescendo.
N.V.: Carbs: 20g, Protein: 5g, Fats: 4g, Fiber: 4g, Sugar: 5g.

Recipe 8: Okra Opera Ovation

P.T.: 25 minutes
Ingr.: Okra ode, tomato tableau, onion oratory, cumin cinema.
Serves: 3
M. of C.: Stir-fried

Process: Orchestrate okra with tomato tones and onion opera. Conclude with cumin cadences.
N.V.: Carbs: 10g, Protein: 3g, Fats: 5g, Fiber: 3g, Sugar: 3g.

Recipe 9: Kale Keynote Kudos

P.T.: 20 minutes

Ingr.: Kale chronicle, garlic galaxy, chili chorus, lemon limelight.

Serves: 3
M. of C.: Wilted
Process: Whisk kale with garlic glints. Chronicle with chili canticles and a lemon lilt.

N.V.: Carbs: 7g, Protein: 4g, Fats: 4g, Fiber: 3g, Sugar: 2g.

Recipe 10: Butternut Ballet Burlesque

P.T.: 40 minutes
Ingr.: Butternut ballad, rosemary rhapsody, garlic galaxy, olive opera.
Serves: 4
M. of C.: Roasted

Process: Breathe life into butternut beats with rosemary refrains. Glisten with garlic and olive overture.
N.V.: Carbs: 15g, Protein: 2g, Fats: 6g, Fiber: 4g, Sugar: 4g.

Vegetarian

Recipe 1: Tofu and Tomato Fusion

P.T.: 30 minutes
Ingr.: Firm tofu, sun-dried tomatoes, minced garlic, ginger.
Serves: 4
M. of C.: Pan-Seared

Process: Slice tofu into blocks and marinate with sun-dried tomatoes, minced garlic, and ginger. Pan-sear until golden.
N.V.: Carbs: 4g, Protein: 8g, Fats: 6g, Fiber: 1g, Sugar: 2g.

Recipe 2: Lentil and Vegetable Stew

P.T.: 50 minutes

Ingr.: Green lentils, diced tomatoes, chopped carrots, ground cumin.
Serves: 4
M. of C.: Simmered
Process: Combine lentils with diced tomatoes, add chopped carrots and sprinkle with ground cumin. Simmer until lentils are soft.
N.V.: Carbs: 45g, Protein: 18g, Fats: 1g, Fiber: 15g, Sugar: 6g.

Recipe 3: Chickpea and Onion Medley

P.T.: 40 minutes

Ingr.: Chickpeas, diced onions, paprika, ground coriander.

Serves: 4
M. of C.: Stewed
Process: Mix chickpeas and onions, sprinkle with paprika and ground coriander. Stew on medium heat until flavors meld.

N.V.: Carbs: 34g, Protein: 12g, Fats: 4g, Fiber: 10g, Sugar: 6g.

Recipe 4: Sautéed Spinach with Almonds

P.T.: 25 minutes
Ingr.: Fresh spinach, sliced almonds, garlic cloves, feta cheese.
Serves: 3
M. of C.: Sautéed

Process: Sauté spinach and garlic until wilted, top with sliced almonds and crumbled feta.
N.V.: Carbs: 8g, Protein: 9g, Fats: 7g, Fiber: 4g, Sugar: 3g.

Recipe 5: Roasted Butternut Squash

P.T.: 55 minutes
Ingr.: Butternut squash, sage leaves, olive oil, black pepper.
Serves: 4
M. of C.: Roasted

Process: Slice butternut squash, drizzle with olive oil, sprinkle with sage leaves and black pepper. Roast until tender.
N.V.: Carbs: 22g, Protein: 2g, Fats: 6g, Fiber: 6g, Sugar: 5g.

Recipe 6: Eggplant Tomato Bake

P.T.: 40 minutes
Ingr.: Eggplant slices, tomato sauce, fresh basil, mozzarella cheese.
Serves: 4
M. of C.: Baked

Process: Layer eggplant slices with tomato sauce, fresh basil, and mozzarella. Bake until bubbly and golden.
N.V.: Carbs: 15g, Protein: 9g, Fats: 8g, Fiber: 7g, Sugar: 7g.

Recipe 7: Quinoa Salad with Lemon Vinaigrette

P.T.: 35 minutes
Ingr.: Cooked quinoa, bell peppers, corn kernels, lemon zest and juice.
Serves: 4
M. of C.: Tossed

Process: Mix quinoa with chopped bell peppers and corn kernels. Drizzle with a vinaigrette made of lemon zest and juice.
N.V.: Carbs: 34g, Protein: 8g, Fats: 3g, Fiber: 5g, Sugar: 4g.

Recipe 8: Cauliflower Stir-Fry with Turmeric

P.T.: 30 minutes

Ingr.: Cauliflower florets, ground turmeric, sliced almonds, olive oil.

Serves: 4
M. of C.: Stir-fried
Process: Stir-fry cauliflower florets in olive oil, sprinkle with turmeric, and finish with sliced almonds for crunch.

N.V.: Carbs: 12g, Protein: 6g, Fats: 8g, Fiber: 5g, Sugar: 4g.

Recipe 9: Grilled Portobello Mushrooms

P.T.: 20 minutes
Ingr.: Portobello mushroom caps, olive oil, minced garlic, chopped parsley.
Serves: 2
M. of C.: Grilled

Process: Brush mushroom caps with olive oil and minced garlic. Grill until tender. Garnish with chopped parsley.
N.V.: Carbs: 6g, Protein: 2g, Fats: 5g, Fiber: 2g, Sugar: 3g.

Recipe 10: Tempeh and Broccoli Stir-Fry

P.T.: 30 minutes
Ingr.: Tempeh cubes, broccoli florets, soy sauce (low-sodium), ground ginger.
Serves: 4
M. of C.: Stir-fried

Process: Sauté tempeh cubes until browned. Add broccoli florets and stir in a mix of soy sauce and ground ginger. Cook until broccoli is tender yet crisp.
N.V.: Carbs: 16g, Protein: 18g, Fats: 7g, Fiber: 5g, Sugar: 3g.

Recipe 11: Zucchini Boats with Ricotta Filling

P.T.: 40 minutes
Ingr.: Zucchini halves, ricotta cheese, chopped tomatoes, minced basil.
Serves: 4
M. of C.: Baked

Process: Scoop out the center of zucchini halves. Mix ricotta cheese, chopped tomatoes, and basil. Fill zucchini with the mixture and bake until tender.
N.V.: Carbs: 10g, Protein: 8g, Fats: 6g, Fiber: 3g, Sugar: 4g.

Recipe 12: Brussels Sprouts and Walnut Sauté

P.T.: 25 minutes
Ingr.: Brussels sprouts, chopped walnuts, garlic cloves, olive oil.
Serves: 4
M. of C.: Sautéed

Process: Sauté Brussels sprouts in olive oil until golden. Mix in garlic and walnuts and cook until fragrant.
N.V.: Carbs: 12g, Protein: 6g, Fats: 9g, Fiber: 4g, Sugar: 3g.

Recipe 13: Spaghetti Squash with Herbs

P.T.: 50 minutes
Ingr.: Spaghetti squash, mixed fresh herbs, garlic cloves, olive oil.
Serves: 4
M. of C.: Roasted

Process: Halve and seed the spaghetti squash. Roast until tender. Scrape out the strands and toss with herbs, garlic, and olive oil.
N.V.: Carbs: 10g, Protein: 2g, Fats: 7g, Fiber: 2g, Sugar: 4g.

Recipe 14: Ratatouille Medley

P.T.: 1 hour
Ingr.: Eggplant, zucchini, bell peppers, diced tomatoes, thyme.
Serves: 4
M. of C.: Simmered

Process: Dice vegetables uniformly. In a pot, combine all ingredients and simmer until flavors meld and vegetables are tender.
N.V.: Carbs: 22g, Protein: 5g, Fats: 1g, Fiber: 8g, Sugar: 12g.

Recipe 15: Vegan Cauliflower Pizza

P.T.: 1 hour
Ingr.: Cauliflower rice, flaxseed meal, tomato sauce, assorted vegetable toppings.
Serves: 2
M. of C.: Baked

Process: Combine cauliflower rice and flaxseed meal to form a dough. Press on a baking sheet. Bake until set, top with sauce and veggies, and bake again until crispy.
N.V.: Carbs: 30g, Protein: 7g, Fats: 5g, Fiber: 10g, Sugar: 6g.

Recipe 16: Quinoa and Vegetable Medley

P.T.: 35 minutes
Ingr.: Quinoa, bell peppers, zucchini, cherry tomatoes, olive oil.
Serves: 4
M. of C.: Sautéed

Process: Cook quinoa as directed. In a separate pan, sauté bell peppers, zucchini, and cherry tomatoes in olive oil until tender. Mix with quinoa and serve.
N.V.: Carbs: 35g, Protein: 8g, Fats: 7g, Fiber: 5g, Sugar: 4g.

Recipe 17: Stuffed Bell Peppers

P.T.: 1 hour
Ingr.: Bell peppers, black beans, corn, diced tomatoes, cumin.
Serves: 4
M. of C.: Baked

Process: Hollow out bell peppers. Mix black beans, corn, diced tomatoes, and cumin. Fill the peppers with this mixture. Bake until peppers are tender.
N.V.: Carbs: 45g, Protein: 13g, Fats: 2g, Fiber: 12g, Sugar: 8g.

Recipe 18: Butternut Squash and Tofu Curry

P.T.: 40 minutes
Ingr.: Butternut squash, tofu cubes, coconut milk, curry powder.
Serves: 4
M. of C.: Simmered

Process: Sauté butternut squash and tofu cubes until golden. Add coconut milk and curry powder. Simmer until squash is tender.
N.V.: Carbs: 40g, Protein: 15g, Fats: 10g, Fiber: 7g, Sugar: 6g.

Recipe 19: Eggplant and Chickpea Stew

P.T.: 50 minutes
Ingr.: Eggplant, chickpeas, diced tomatoes, coriander.
Serves: 4
M. of C.: Stewed

Process: Dice eggplant into cubes. Combine eggplant, chickpeas, diced tomatoes, and coriander in a pot. Stew until eggplant is tender.
N.V.: Carbs: 50g, Protein: 12g, Fats: 3g, Fiber: 15g, Sugar: 10g.

Recipe 20: Mushroom and Spinach Frittata

P.T.: 30 minutes
Ingr.: Mushrooms, spinach, egg whites, olive oil, garlic.
Serves: 4
M. of C.: Oven-baked

Process: Sauté mushrooms, spinach, and garlic in olive oil. Pour in whisked egg whites and transfer to the oven. Bake until set.
N.V.: Carbs: 8g, Protein: 10g, Fats: 7g, Fiber: 2g, Sugar: 3g.

Salads

Recipe 1: Kale and Walnut Delight

Ingr.: Curly kale, walnuts, olive oil, lemon juice, chia seeds.
Serves: 4
M. of C.: Tossed
Process: De-stem kale and tear into bite-size pieces. Mix with walnuts, chia seeds, olive oil, and fresh lemon juice. Toss well to combine.
N.V.: Carbs: 12g, Protein: 5g, Fats: 15g, Fiber: 4g, Sugar: 0g.

P.T.: 15 minutes

Recipe 2: Spinach and Feta Toss

P.T.: 10 minutes
Ingr.: Fresh spinach, feta cheese, sun-dried tomatoes, pumpkin seeds.
Serves: 3
M. of C.: Tossed

Process: Combine spinach, crumbled feta, sun-dried tomatoes, and pumpkin seeds. Toss gently to mix.
N.V.: Carbs: 6g, Protein: 7g, Fats: 8g, Fiber: 2g, Sugar: 2g.

Recipe 3: Chickpea and Cucumber Mix

P.T.: 15 minutes
Ingr.: Chickpeas, cucumber, olive oil, apple cider vinegar, fresh mint.
Serves: 4
M. of C.: Tossed

Process: Dice cucumber. Combine with chickpeas, finely chopped mint, olive oil, and vinegar. Stir to combine.
N.V.: Carbs: 30g, Protein: 8g, Fats: 5g, Fiber: 7g, Sugar: 4g.

Recipe 4: Grilled Asparagus and Quinoa Bowl

P.T.: 25 minutes
Ingr.: Asparagus, quinoa, lemon zest, olive oil.
Serves: 4
M. of C.: Grilled

Process: Grill asparagus until tender. Mix with cooked quinoa, lemon zest, and a drizzle of olive oil.
N.V.: Carbs: 35g, Protein: 7g, Fats: 8g, Fiber: 4g, Sugar: 2g.

Recipe 5: Beetroot and Goat Cheese Platter

P.T.: 20 minutes
Ingr.: Beets, goat cheese, arugula, hazelnuts.
Serves: 4
M. of C.: Tossed
Process: Roast or steam beets until tender. Slice and arrange on a platter with arugula.

Sprinkle with crumbled goat cheese and hazelnuts.
N.V.: Carbs: 18g, Protein: 6g, Fats: 8g, Fiber: 4g, Sugar: 12g.

Recipe 6: Avocado and Tomato Salsa Salad

P.T.: 10 minutes
Ingr.: Avocado, cherry tomatoes, lime juice, cilantro.
Serves: 3
M. of C.: Tossed

Process: Dice avocado and halve cherry tomatoes. Mix with fresh lime juice and chopped cilantro.
N.V.: Carbs: 15g, Protein: 2g, Fats: 14g, Fiber: 7g, Sugar: 4g.

Recipe 7: Mediterranean Tuna Salad

P.T.: 20 minutes
Ingr.: Tuna, mixed olives, capers, romaine lettuce, olive oil.
Serves: 4
M. of C.: Tossed

Process: Flake tuna and mix with chopped olives, capers, and sliced romaine lettuce. Dress with olive oil.
N.V.: Carbs: 5g, Protein: 20g, Fats: 15g, Fiber: 2g, Sugar: 1g.

Recipe 8: Cabbage and Apple Slaw

P.T.: 15 minutes
Ingr.: Green cabbage, red apple, sunflower seeds, apple cider vinegar.
Serves: 4
M. of C.: Tossed

Process: Shred cabbage and thinly slice apple. Mix with sunflower seeds and dress with vinegar.
N.V.: Carbs: 15g, Protein: 3g, Fats: 5g, Fiber: 4g, Sugar: 10g.

Recipe 9: Zesty Broccoli and Carrot Salad

P.T.: 15 minutes
Ingr.: Broccoli florets, grated carrot, almonds, olive oil, lemon juice.
Serves: 4
M. of C.: Tossed

Process: Blanche broccoli until just tender. Mix with grated carrot, sliced almonds, olive oil, and fresh lemon juice.
N.V.: Carbs: 12g, Protein: 5g, Fats: 10g, Fiber: 4g, Sugar: 3g.

Recipe 10: Fennel and Citrus Burst

P.T.: 15 minutes
Ingr.: Fennel bulb, oranges, olive oil, black olives.
Serves: 4
M. of C.: Tossed

Process: Thinly slice fennel bulb and segment oranges. Combine with sliced black olives and dress with a splash of olive oil.
N.V.: Carbs: 18g, Protein: 2g, Fats: 7g, Fiber: 4g, Sugar: 12g.

Recipe 11: Radish and Cucumber Crunch

P.T.: 10 minutes
Ingr.: Radishes, cucumber, dill, white wine vinegar.
Serves: 4
M. of C.: Tossed

Process: Thinly slice radishes and cucumber. Toss with chopped dill and drizzle with white wine vinegar.
N.V.: Carbs: 5g, Protein: 1g, Fats: 0.5g, Fiber: 2g, Sugar: 2g.

Recipe 12: Charred Corn and Black Bean Mix

P.T.: 20 minutes
Ingr.: Corn on the cob, black beans, lime zest, cumin.
Serves: 4
M. of C.: Grilled

Process: Char corn on a grill or skillet. Remove kernels and mix with rinsed black beans, lime zest, and a sprinkle of cumin.
N.V.: Carbs: 30g, Protein: 8g, Fats: 2g, Fiber: 7g, Sugar: 4g.

Recipe 13: Jicama and Mango Medley

P.T.: 15 minutes
Ingr.: Jicama, mango, cilantro, lime juice.
Serves: 4
M. of C.: Tossed

Process: Dice jicama and mango. Toss with finely chopped cilantro and a squeeze of fresh lime juice.
N.V.: Carbs: 25g, Protein: 2g, Fats: 0.5g, Fiber: 7g, Sugar: 18g.

Recipe 14: Romaine and Parmesan Pile

P.T.: 10 minutes
Ingr.: Romaine lettuce, Parmesan shavings, olive oil, lemon juice.
Serves: 4
M. of C.: Tossed

Process: Tear romaine leaves into bite-sized pieces. Drizzle with a mix of olive oil and lemon juice, then sprinkle with Parmesan shavings.
N.V.: Carbs: 3g, Protein: 6g, Fats: 8g, Fiber: 2g, Sugar: 1g.

Recipe 15: Grapefruit and Arugula Fusion

P.T.: 15 minutes
Ingr.: Grapefruit, arugula, toasted walnuts, balsamic reduction.
Serves: 4
M. of C.: Tossed

Process: Segment grapefruit and toss with arugula. Top with toasted walnuts and a drizzle of balsamic reduction.
N.V.: Carbs: 15g, Protein: 4g, Fats: 8g, Fiber: 3g, Sugar: 9g.

Recipe 16: Snow Pea and Bell Pepper Mix

P.T.: 15 minutes
Ingr.: Snow peas, bell peppers (multi-colored), sesame seeds, sesame oil.
Serves: 4
M. of C.: Sautéed

Process: Sauté snow peas and thinly sliced bell peppers in a touch of sesame oil. Finish with a sprinkle of toasted sesame seeds.
N.V.: Carbs: 12g, Protein: 3g, Fats: 4g, Fiber: 4g, Sugar: 6g.

Recipe 17: Pineapple and Mint Zest

P.T.: 10 minutes
Ingr.: Fresh pineapple, mint leaves, chia seeds.
Serves: 4
M. of C.: Tossed

Process: Dice pineapple. Mix with finely chopped mint leaves and sprinkle with chia seeds.
N.V.: Carbs: 22g, Protein: 1g, Fats: 2g, Fiber: 3g, Sugar: 18g.

Recipe 18: Watercress and Pomegranate Pleaser

P.T.: 10 minutes
Ingr.: Watercress, pomegranate seeds, olive oil, lemon zest.
Serves: 4
M. of C.: Tossed

Process: Mix watercress with pomegranate seeds. Drizzle with olive oil and sprinkle with freshly grated lemon zest.
N.V.: Carbs: 8g, Protein: 2g, Fats: 5g, Fiber: 2g, Sugar: 5g.

Recipe 19: Asparagus and Goat Cheese Mingle

P.T.: 20 minutes
Ingr.: Asparagus spears, goat cheese, slivered almonds, Dijon mustard.
Serves: 4
M. of C.: Grilled

Process: Grill asparagus spears until tender. Serve topped with crumbled goat cheese, toasted slivered almonds, and a Dijon mustard drizzle.
N.V.: Carbs: 5g, Protein: 6g, Fats: 8g, Fiber: 2g, Sugar: 2g.

Recipe 20: Beet and Feta Fusion

P.T.: 45 minutes (including beet roasting time)
Ingr.: Beets, feta cheese, parsley, olive oil, red wine vinegar.
Serves: 4
M. of C.: Roasted

Process: Roast beets until tender. Once cooled, peel and dice them. Combine in a bowl with crumbled feta and chopped parsley. Dress with a mix of olive oil and red wine vinegar.
N.V.: Carbs: 13g, Protein: 4g, Fats: 6g, Fiber: 3g, Sugar: 9g.

Sides

Recipe 1: Zucchini and Lemon Sautee

P.T.: 15 minutes
Ingr.: Zucchini, olive oil, lemon zest, lemon juice, salt.
Serves: 4
M. of C.: Sautéed

Process: Slice zucchini thinly. Heat olive oil in a pan and sauté zucchini until tender. Sprinkle lemon zest and a splash of lemon juice. Season with salt.
N.V.: Carbs: 4g, Protein: 1g, Fats: 4g, Fiber: 1g, Sugar: 2g.

Recipe 2: Cilantro Lime Cauliflower Rice

Ingr.: Cauliflower, cilantro, lime juice, olive oil, salt.
Serves: 4
M. of C.: Pan-fried
Process: Pulse cauliflower in a blender until rice-like. Heat olive oil in a skillet, add cauliflower rice and cook until tender. Stir in chopped cilantro and lime juice.
N.V.: Carbs: 5g, Protein: 2g, Fats: 5g, Fiber: 2g, Sugar: 2g.

P.T.: 20 minutes

Recipe 3: Green Beans Almondine

P.T.: 20 minutes
Ingr.: Green beans, almonds, butter, garlic, lemon juice.
Serves: 4
M. of C.: Sauteed

Process: Sauté almonds in butter until golden. Add finely chopped garlic and green beans. Cook until beans are al dente. Drizzle with lemon juice.
N.V.: Carbs: 8g, Protein: 3g, Fats: 9g, Fiber: 3g, Sugar: 4g.

Recipe 4: Roasted Brussels Sprouts with Pecans

P.T.: 35 minutes
Ingr.: Brussels sprouts, pecans, olive oil, salt, black pepper.
Serves: 4
M. of C.: Roasted

Process: Toss Brussels sprouts in olive oil, salt, and pepper. Roast until golden. Mix in toasted pecans before serving.
N.V.: Carbs: 12g, Protein: 4g, Fats: 10g, Fiber: 4g, Sugar: 2g.

Recipe 5: Lemon Herb Asparagus

P.T.: 15 minutes

Ingr.: Asparagus, olive oil, lemon zest, rosemary, thyme, salt.

Serves: 4

M. of C.: Grilled

Process: Toss asparagus in olive oil, lemon zest, and herbs. Grill until tender. Season with salt.

N.V.: Carbs: 4g, Protein: 2g, Fats: 5g, Fiber: 2g, Sugar: 2g.

Recipe 6: Garlic Parmesan Broccoli

P.T.: 20 minutes

Ingr.: Broccoli florets, olive oil, garlic, Parmesan cheese, salt.

Serves: 4

M. of C.: Roasted

Process: Toss broccoli in olive oil and minced garlic. Roast until crispy. Sprinkle with grated Parmesan cheese.

N.V.: Carbs: 6g, Protein: 5g, Fats: 8g, Fiber: 3g, Sugar: 2g.

Recipe 7: Sesame Snow Peas

P.T.: 10 minutes

Ingr.: Snow peas, sesame oil, sesame seeds, soy sauce (low sodium).

Serves: 4

M. of C.: Sautéed

Process: Sauté snow peas in sesame oil for 3-4 minutes. Add a splash of soy sauce and sprinkle with sesame seeds.

N.V.: Carbs: 6g, Protein: 2g, Fats: 4g, Fiber: 2g, Sugar: 3g.

Recipe 8: Herb Marinated Mushrooms

P.T.: 20 minutes (plus marinating)

Ingr.: Mushrooms, olive oil, vinegar, rosemary, oregano, garlic, salt.

Serves: 4

M. of C.: Marinated

Process: Combine all ingredients and let mushrooms marinate for at least 2 hours. Serve chilled.

N.V.: Carbs: 4g, Protein: 2g, Fats: 7g, Fiber: 1g, Sugar: 2g.

Recipe 9: Spiced Roasted Butternut Squash

P.T.: 40 minutes

Ingr.: Butternut squash, olive oil, cumin, smoked paprika, salt.

Serves: 4

M. of C.: Roasted

Process: Cube butternut squash and toss in spices and olive oil. Roast until tender and slightly caramelized.

N.V.: Carbs: 15g, Protein: 1g, Fats: 5g, Fiber: 2g, Sugar: 3g.

Recipe 10: Toasted Almond & Cranberry Quinoa

P.T.: 25 minutes

Ingr.: Quinoa, almonds, dried cranberries (unsweetened), olive oil, salt.
Serves: 4
M. of C.: Boiled

Process: Cook quinoa as directed. Stir in toasted almonds, cranberries, and a splash of olive oil. Season with salt.
N.V.: Carbs: 23g, Protein: 6g, Fats: 8g, Fiber: 3g, Sugar: 5g.

Recipe 11: Herb-Stuffed Artichokes

P.T.: 50 minutes
Ingr.: Artichokes, garlic, parsley, basil, olive oil, lemon juice, salt.
Serves: 4
M. of C.: Steamed

Process: Halve artichokes, remove the choke. Mix garlic, parsley, and basil with olive oil and lemon juice. Drizzle over the artichokes. Steam until tender.
N.V.: Carbs: 17g, Protein: 5g, Fats: 7g, Fiber: 7g, Sugar: 2g.

Recipe 12: Spinach and Feta Stuffed Tomatoes

P.T.: 30 minutes
Ingr.: Tomatoes, spinach, feta cheese, olive oil, garlic, salt.
Serves: 4
M. of C.: Baked

Process: Hollow out tomatoes. Sauté spinach and garlic in olive oil. Mix with crumbled feta. Stuff tomatoes and bake until soft.
N.V.: Carbs: 6g, Protein: 4g, Fats: 6g, Fiber: 2g, Sugar: 3g.

Recipe 13: Balsamic Glazed Eggplant

P.T.: 25 minutes
Ingr.: Eggplant, balsamic vinegar, olive oil, garlic, salt.
Serves: 4
M. of C.: Grilled

Process: Slice eggplant, brush with olive oil and grill until charred. Drizzle with balsamic reduction.
N.V.: Carbs: 12g, Protein: 1g, Fats: 5g, Fiber: 5g, Sugar: 7g.

Recipe 14: Ginger-Sesame Edamame

P.T.: 10 minutes
Ingr.: Edamame, sesame oil, ginger, salt.
Serves: 4
M. of C.: Steamed

Process: Steam edamame. Toss with sesame oil and grated ginger. Season with salt.
N.V.: Carbs: 8g, Protein: 9g, Fats: 5g, Fiber: 4g, Sugar: 2g.

Recipe 15: Garlic Lemon Roasted Okra

P.T.: 20 minutes

Ingr.: Okra, olive oil, garlic, lemon zest, salt.

Serves: 4
M. of C.: Roasted
Process: Toss okra in olive oil, minced garlic, and lemon zest. Roast until crispy.

N.V.: Carbs: 7g, Protein: 2g, Fats: 5g, Fiber: 3g, Sugar: 1g.

Recipe 16: Thyme-Roasted Radishes

P.T.: 25 minutes
Ingr.: Radishes, olive oil, fresh thyme, salt.
Serves: 4
M. of C.: Roasted

Process: Toss halved radishes in olive oil and thyme. Roast until tender and slightly caramelized.

N.V.: Carbs: 4g, Protein: 1g, Fats: 5g, Fiber: 2g, Sugar: 2g.

Recipe 17: Grilled Asparagus with Almond Pesto

P.T.: 20 minutes
Ingr.: Asparagus, almonds, basil, garlic, olive oil, salt.
Serves: 4
M. of C.: Grilled

Process: Grill asparagus until tender. Pulse almonds, basil, garlic, and olive oil in a blender to create pesto. Drizzle over asparagus.

N.V.: Carbs: 6g, Protein: 4g, Fats: 9g, Fiber: 2g, Sugar: 2g.

Recipe 18: Turmeric-Cauliflower Steaks

P.T.: 30 minutes
Ingr.: Cauliflower, turmeric powder, olive oil, black pepper, salt.
Serves: 4
M. of C.: Roasted

Process: Cut cauliflower into steaks. Brush with a mix of olive oil, turmeric, salt, and black pepper. Roast until golden.

N.V.: Carbs: 8g, Protein: 3g, Fats: 6g, Fiber: 3g, Sugar: 3g.

Recipe 19: Cumin-Dusted Roasted Carrots

P.T.: 35 minutes
Ingr.: Carrots, olive oil, cumin powder, salt.
Serves: 4
M. of C.: Roasted

Process: Toss carrots in olive oil, cumin, and salt. Roast until caramelized.

N.V.: Carbs: 10g, Protein: 1g, Fats: 5g, Fiber: 3g, Sugar: 5g.

Recipe 20: Zucchini Ribbons with Lemon and Parsley

P.T.: 10 minutes
Ingr.: Zucchini, lemon zest, parsley, olive oil, salt.

Serves: 4
M. of C.: Raw

Process: Use a vegetable peeler to create thin ribbons of zucchini. Toss with lemon zest, chopped parsley, olive oil, and salt.

N.V.: Carbs: 4g, Protein: 2g, Fats: 5g, Fiber: 1g, Sugar: 2g.

Desserts

Recipe 1: Cinnamon Chia Pudding

P.T.: 10 minutes (plus chilling)

Ingr.: Chia seeds, almond milk, cinnamon, stevia, vanilla extract.
Serves: 4
M. of C.: Refrigerated
Process: Combine chia seeds with almond milk, stevia, cinnamon, and vanilla. Let sit in the refrigerator until thickened.
N.V.: Carbs: 10g, Protein: 4g, Fats: 8g, Fiber: 8g, Sugar: 0g.

Recipe 2: Dark Chocolate Avocado Mousse

P.T.: 15 minutes
Ingr.: Avocado, dark cocoa powder, stevia, vanilla extract.
Serves: 2
M. of C.: Blended

Process: Blend avocado with cocoa powder, stevia, and vanilla until smooth. Chill before serving.
N.V.: Carbs: 8g, Protein: 2g, Fats: 15g, Fiber: 6g, Sugar: 0g.

Recipe 3: Lemon Coconut Bars

P.T.: 35 minutes
Ingr.: Almond flour, coconut flakes, lemon zest, eggs, stevia.
Serves: 8
M. of C.: Baked

Process: Mix ingredients and press into a baking dish. Bake until firm.
N.V.: Carbs: 6g, Protein: 4g, Fats: 10g, Fiber: 3g, Sugar: 0g.

Recipe 4: Raspberry Almond Clusters

P.T.: 20 minutes
Ingr.: Fresh raspberries, unsweetened dark chocolate, toasted almonds.
Serves: 6

M. of C.: Chilled
Process: Melt chocolate and mix with almonds. Place a raspberry in the center of each almond cluster. Chill until set.

N.V.: Carbs: 7g, Protein: 3g, Fats: 8g, Fiber: 4g, Sugar: 2g.

Recipe 5: Vanilla Ricotta Crème

P.T.: 10 minutes
Ingr.: Ricotta cheese, stevia, vanilla extract.
Serves: 4
M. of C.: Mixed

Process: Combine ricotta with stevia and vanilla. Serve chilled.
N.V.: Carbs: 4g, Protein: 8g, Fats: 6g, Fiber: 0g, Sugar: 1g.

Recipe 6: Blackberry Ginger Gelatin

P.T.: 10 minutes (plus setting time)
Ingr.: Fresh blackberries, ginger, gelatin, stevia.
Serves: 4
M. of C.: Refrigerated

Process: Heat blackberries and ginger. Strain, mix in gelatin and stevia, and let set in the refrigerator.
N.V.: Carbs: 5g, Protein: 3g, Fats: 0g, Fiber: 3g, Sugar: 2g.

Recipe 7: Pecan-Stuffed Baked Apples

P.T.: 40 minutes
Ingr.: Green apples, pecans, cinnamon, stevia.
Serves: 4
M. of C.: Baked

Process: Hollow apples, mix pecans with cinnamon and stevia, stuff apples, and bake.
N.V.: Carbs: 15g, Protein: 2g, Fats: 8g, Fiber: 4g, Sugar: 9g.

Recipe 8: Creamy Peanut Butter Fudge

P.T.: 10 minutes (plus chilling)
Ingr.: Natural peanut butter, coconut oil, stevia.
Serves: 8
M. of C.: Refrigerated

Process: Melt coconut oil, mix with peanut butter and stevia. Pour into molds and chill.
N.V.: Carbs: 3g, Protein: 4g, Fats: 12g, Fiber: 1g, Sugar: 0g.

Recipe 9: Mocha Chia Seed Brownies

P.T.: 40 minutes
Ingr.: Chia seeds, almond flour, dark cocoa powder, espresso powder, stevia, eggs.
Serves: 8
M. of C.: Baked

Process: Combine dry and wet ingredients separately, then mix together. Pour into a baking dish and bake.
N.V.: Carbs: 9g, Protein: 5g, Fats: 8g, Fiber: 5g, Sugar: 0g.

Recipe 10: Spiced Pumpkin Custard

P.T.: 45 minutes
Ingr.: Canned pumpkin, eggs, heavy cream, cinnamon, nutmeg, stevia.
Serves: 4
M. of C.: Baked

Process: Mix ingredients and pour into ramekins. Bake in a water bath until set.
N.V.: Carbs: 8g, Protein: 5g, Fats: 12g, Fiber: 3g, Sugar: 3g.

Recipe 11: Coconut Almond Bites

P.T.: 20 minutes (plus chilling)
Ingr.: Unsweetened shredded coconut, almond butter, stevia, vanilla extract.
Serves: 12
M. of C.: Refrigerated

Process: Mix all ingredients in a bowl. Form small balls and refrigerate until firm.
N.V.: Carbs: 5g, Protein: 3g, Fats: 10g, Fiber: 2g, Sugar: 1g.

Recipe 12: Cacao Nib and Hazelnut Crunch

P.T.: 15 minutes
Ingr.: Cacao nibs, hazelnuts, stevia.
Serves: 6
M. of C.: No-cook

Process: Mix cacao nibs with roasted hazelnuts. Sprinkle stevia for added sweetness.
N.V.: Carbs: 6g, Protein: 4g, Fats: 12g, Fiber: 3g, Sugar: 0g.

Recipe 13: Strawberry Cheesecake Cups

P.T.: 25 minutes
Ingr.: Cream cheese, strawberries, almond flour, stevia, lemon juice.
Serves: 6
M. of C.: Refrigerated

Process: Layer a mix of almond flour and stevia at the bottom of cups. Blend strawberries, cream cheese, and lemon juice. Pour over the base and chill.
N.V.: Carbs: 7g, Protein: 4g, Fats: 11g, Fiber: 1g, Sugar: 3g.

Recipe 14: Blueberry Lemon Gelatin Cups

P.T.: 15 minutes (plus setting time)
Ingr.: Fresh blueberries, lemon zest, gelatin, stevia.
Serves: 4
M. of C.: Refrigerated

Process: Heat blueberries until they release juice. Add lemon zest, stevia, and gelatin. Pour into cups and refrigerate until set.
N.V.: Carbs: 6g, Protein: 3g, Fats: 0g, Fiber: 2g, Sugar: 3g.

Recipe 15: Keto Chocolate Avocado Truffles

P.T.: 20 minutes (plus chilling)
Ingr.: Avocado, dark cocoa powder, stevia, cacao nibs.
Serves: 10
M. of C.: Refrigerated

Process: Blend avocado with cocoa powder and stevia until smooth. Form into balls and roll in cacao nibs. Chill.
N.V.: Carbs: 4g, Protein: 2g, Fats: 8g, Fiber: 3g, Sugar: 0g.

Recipe 16: Creamy Raspberry Coconut Pops

P.T.: 10 minutes (plus freezing)
Ingr.: Fresh raspberries, full-fat coconut milk, stevia.
Serves: 6
M. of C.: Frozen

Process: Blend raspberries with coconut milk and stevia. Pour into popsicle molds and freeze.
N.V.: Carbs: 6g, Protein: 2g, Fats: 10g, Fiber: 2g, Sugar: 2g.

Recipe 17: Zesty Lime Meringue Cups

P.T.: 45 minutes
Ingr.: Eggs, lime zest, stevia.
Serves: 8
M. of C.: Baked

Process: Separate egg yolks and whites. Beat whites with stevia until stiff peaks form. Fold in lime zest. Spoon into cups and bake.
N.V.: Carbs: 1g, Protein: 3g, Fats: 2g, Fiber: 0g, Sugar: 0g.

Recipe 18: Keto Caramel Pudding

P.T.: 20 minutes
Ingr.: Heavy cream, butter, vanilla extract, stevia.
Serves: 4
M. of C.: Stovetop

Process: Melt butter, add heavy cream and stevia. Simmer until thickened. Cool and serve.
N.V.: Carbs: 3g, Protein: 1g, Fats: 18g, Fiber: 0g, Sugar: 1g.

Recipe 19: Cream Cheese Berry Parfait

P.T.: 15 minutes
Ingr.: Cream cheese, mixed berries, almond flakes, stevia.
Serves: 4
M. of C.: Layered

Process: In a glass, layer cream cheese, berries, and almond flakes. Sprinkle with stevia between layers.
N.V.: Carbs: 8g, Protein: 4g, Fats: 10g, Fiber: 2g, Sugar: 4g.

Recipe 20: Almond Joyous Bites

P.T.: 20 minutes (plus chilling)

Ingr.: Unsweetened shredded coconut, almond butter, dark cocoa powder, stevia.

Serves: 12

M. of C.: Refrigerated

Process: Combine all ingredients. Form into small balls. Refrigerate.

N.V.: Carbs: 5g, Protein: 3g, Fats: 11g, Fiber: 2g, Sugar: 1g.

The chapter's collection of recipes is more than simply a how-to manual; it's also a celebration of how food can change people's lives. Each meal serves as evidence that flavor and health don't have to be mutually exclusive. You may indulge in a world of culinary pleasures that are in line with the dietary requirements of someone with Type 2 Diabetes by making strategic decisions about the ingredients you use and how they are prepared. Keep in mind that cooking is an art, and you are encouraged, like all artists, to explore, adapt, and personalize each recipe. With the help of these recipes, you may manage your diabetes while still adopting a way of life that combines wellness and culinary enjoyment. Let these meals serve as both your compass and your companion as you continue on your route to controlling diabetes, serving as a gentle reminder that the way to health may be paved with delectable possibilities.

Chapter 3: 30-Day Meal Plan

Embarking on a culinary journey means not just exploring flavors but also understanding the rhythm of consistent and health-conscious eating. Our 30-day meal plan is designed with this essence in mind, ensuring you are not only tantalized by exotic and delectable dishes but also enveloped in a routine that nourishes your body and soul. Each meal, carefully curated, exemplifies the perfect blend of nutrition and taste. These dishes, crafted with love and science, seek to foster a seamless transition into a balanced diet. Over the next thirty days, as you traverse through these culinary landscapes, allow yourself to delve deep into the nuances of each ingredient, the symphony of flavors, and the joy of savoring food that does good to both your palate and well-being. Let this chapter be your guide, your gastronomic map, as you embark on a month-long voyage through textures, tastes, and tantalizing aromas.

Days 1-10

Day	Breakfast	Page	Lunch	Page	Dinner	Page
1	Quinoa Ambrosia with Blueberries	23	Tomato Basil Soup Euphoria	29	Basil Beef Brocade	32

Day	Breakfast	Page	Lunch	Page	Dinner	Page
2	Florentine Egg Cloud with Feta Crumbles	23	Kale & Sm Tommy Salmon Reveal	24	Zesty Lime Beef Fandango	33
3	Chia & Macadamia Porridge Euphoria	25	Quinoa Spinach Munchies	29	Beef & Quinoa Quest	35
4	Almond Nectar & Chia Toast Elevation	23	Sardine & Olive Tapenade Dawn	25	Balsamic Ballet Pork	38
5	Tofu Brekky Scramble Mirage	24	Ricotta Almond Pancake Surprise	25	Terra Tang Lamb Wraps	40
6	Avocado & Cottage Spread Delight	24	Frittata Fusion with Zucchini Spirals	25	Tarragon Tapestry Chicken Thighs	44
7	Cacao-Chia Serenity Pudding	26	Green Spirulina Smoothie Dreamscape	25	Basil Brine Baked Salmon	48
8	Berries & Seed Medley Awe	26	Beetroot Hummus Embrace	28	Dill Drizzle Cod Ceviche	49
9	Ginger-Melon Refresher Bowl	26	Tomato Twilight Tingle	53	Mushroom Melody Mingle	53
10	Artichoke & Pesto Omelet Hug	26	Beet Hummus Hues	32	Lentil Lyric Lagoon	54

Days 11-20

Day	Breakfast	Page	Lunch	Page	Dinner	Page
11	Turmeric Latte & Walnut-Butter Crescents	26	Red Wine Rhapsody Beef	34	Brussels Brio Ballet	57
12	Miso Breakfast Soup Solace	27	Garlic Gaze Pork Tenderloin	36	Roasted Butternut Squash	60
13	Coconut & Cardamom Smoothie Veil	27	Lemon Lustre Pork Chops	36	Quinoa Salad with Lemon Vinaigrette	60
14	Eggplant & Hummus Breakfast Torte	27	Lavender Lure Lamb Chops	40	Beetroot and Goat Cheese Platter	64
15	Hazelnut & Pear Baked Divinity	27	Berry Bliss Lamb Skewers	41	Jicama and Mango Medley	66
16	Chickpea Crunch Bliss	28	Orange Ovation Lamb Curry	41	Asparagus and Goat Cheese Mingle	67

Day	Breakfast	Page	Lunch	Page	Dinner	Page
17	Zucchini Roll-Ups Caress	28	Tarragon Twilight Lamb Steaks	41	Cilantro Lime Cauliflower Rice	68
18	Lemon Garlic Olives Rhapsody	29	Rhubarb Radiance Lamb Tacos	43	Roasted Brussels Sprouts with Pecans	68
19	Pumpkin Seed Trail	30	Ginger Galaxy Chicken Soup	45	Garlic Parmesan Broccoli	69
20	Herb-Infused Cottage Cheese Brilliance	30	Mint Motif Chicken Tacos	46	Sesame Snow Peas	69

Days 21-30

Day	Breakfast	Page	Lunch	Page	Dinner	Page
21	Kale Chips Cascade	30	Cilantro Cynosure Chicken Salad	44	Cumin Concert Calamari Rings	52
22	Tangy Tomato Bruschetta Overture	30	Sage Symphony Chicken Wraps	45	Lavender Lure Lobster Linguine	51
23	Apricot Apprise	31	Peppered Passion Chicken Pizza	47	Lobster and Lemon Grass Luxury	50
24	Fermented Vegetable Frisk	31	Marjoram Marvel Chicken Pot Pie	49	Lobster and Avocado Divinity	49
25	Chocolate & Raspberry Rendezvous	31	Rosemary Rendition Chicken Ramen	50	Almond-Accented Lobster Salad	50
26	Mango & Quinoa Meditation	31	Thyme Thought Chicken Quesadillas	51	Lobster and Pineapple Pilaf	51
27	Apple & Almond Enchantment	32	Turmeric Trace Chicken Tikka Masala	52	Lobster & Lime Loaf	50
28	Berries & Cream Cuddle	33	Fennel Fancy Chicken Tenders	52	Lemongrass Lobster Lasagna	50
29	Grilled Grapefruit & Mint Moment	34	Oregano Odyssey Chicken Omelette	53	Lobster & Lemon Risotto	51
30	Almond-Stuffed Dates Serenade	35	Ginger Gusto Grilled Grouper	54	Lobster and Lentil Lure	51

As we close this chapter of our 30-day meal plan, it's essential to reflect on the journey we've undertaken. Each meal was an experience, a story, a moment where culinary arts met nutritional science. Beyond the delightful tastes and enticing aromas, the essence of this plan was to instill a disciplined yet delicious eating routine, which we hope has now become an integral part of your life. These recipes were not just about satiating hunger but fostering a relationship with food that is both wholesome and indulgent. As you move forward, carry with you the lessons and flavors of this month. Let them be the foundation upon which you build your culinary explorations. And remember, while this chapter concludes, the journey of delightful eating never truly ends. Embrace it with open arms and a curious palate, and may your dining table always be a tableau of colors, health, and joy.

Chapter 4: Conclusion

In the tapestry of life, our habits, choices, and actions weave the intricate patterns that define who we are and who we strive to become. As we stand at the crossroads of this profound journey, our relationship with food emerges not merely as a means of sustenance but as a celebration of life, culture, memories, and shared moments. With every bite, we explore histories, geographies, traditions, and the sacred bond that ties us to this vast universe.

Yet, often, in the clamor of our fast-paced lives, the profound significance of food becomes muffled, shadowed by the transient pleasure of instant gratification. We find ourselves lost in a maze of convenience, forgetting that every meal is an opportunity to connect, to revitalize, to journey through the palimpsest of flavors and memories that our ancestors passed down through generations.

Within the sacred geometry of gastronomy, the art of cooking is akin to alchemy. Transforming humble ingredients into culinary masterpieces demands more than just skill—it requires passion, intuition, and an unerring commitment to the craft. It's a symphony where the notes of taste, texture, and aroma harmonize to birth experiences that linger, not just on our palates, but deep within the realms of our souls.

Indeed, the kitchen becomes a sanctuary, a realm where chaos finds order, where creativity unfurls its wings, and where the tangible meets the ethereal. And, as with any art, it's not just about the final product but the journey—the dance of flames, the rhythm of boiling pots, the alchemical transformations, and the sheer joy of witnessing raw ingredients metamorphose into delectable masterpieces.

Yet, it isn't merely about gourmet delights or exotic flavors. It's about understanding the intimate relationship between food and well-being. How the choices we make in the kitchen reverberate through our lives, shaping our health, mood, and vitality. To truly embrace the gift of food is to understand that every morsel we consume is a choice—a choice that impacts not just our bodies but our environment, society, and the world at large.

Consider, for instance, the ripple effect of choosing a locally sourced apple over one shipped from halfway across the globe. Beyond the burst of flavor that a fresh apple promises, this choice is an ode to sustainability, a nod to local farmers, a step towards reducing carbon footprints, and a commitment to fostering communities. Such seemingly simple choices encapsulate the magic and power of mindful eating.

But how do we navigate this vast, often overwhelming culinary landscape? By honoring the age-old wisdom of our forebears, yet marrying it with the innovations of contemporary times. By understanding that our kitchens are both laboratories and temples, where science meets spirituality. By recognizing that cooking is not a chore but a meditative practice, a form of self-expression, an act of love.

As we've journeyed together through this exploration of food, the underlying ethos has been clear—food, in its essence, is life. It's the stories of our grandparents, the aroma that wafts from our childhood kitchens, the shared laughter over a family dinner, the comfort of a warm soup on a cold evening, the exhilaration of trying something utterly unfamiliar. It's the thread that binds us to our roots, while also allowing us to explore the vast tapestry of global cultures.

In conclusion, as you move forward, let the spirit of this exploration guide you. Let every meal be an adventure, every ingredient a story, every dish an artwork. Recognize the sacred in the mundane, the extraordinary in the ordinary. Let the act of eating be not just about filling your stomach, but nourishing your soul, enriching your experiences, and celebrating the myriad wonders of life.

Remember, in the grand mosaic of existence, our choices, habits, and passions carve out our unique niches. And as you stand, fork and knife in hand, at the threshold of countless culinary adventures, remember that you aren't just consuming food—you're partaking in the eternal dance of life, love, culture, and connection. So, embrace it with zeal, passion, and an insatiable curiosity.

For, in the words of the great Jean Anthelme Brillat-Savarin, "The discovery of a new dish does more for the happiness of the human race than the discovery of a star."

Bon Appétit!

BONUS - The Journey Continues

BONUS

Integrating Physical Exercise and Good Dietary Habits

When dealing with Type 2 diabetes, two essential pillars stand out: physical exercise and good dietary habits. Together, they form a robust foundation for managing and even reversing the impacts of this condition. Let's delve deeper into how intertwining these elements can significantly enhance our health journey.

Physical activity is more than just burning calories; it's about enhancing our body's overall function. Regular exercise improves insulin sensitivity. This means our body needs less insulin to move sugar into our cells. The less insulin we need, the better, as high insulin levels can lead to a series of complications over time. Whether it's a simple walk, jogging, swimming, or weight lifting, each form of exercise plays its role in pushing our bodily systems to work more efficiently.

On the other side of this equation, we have dietary habits. What we consume daily has a direct impact on our blood sugar levels, insulin production, and overall metabolic health. A diet rich in whole foods—comprising whole grains, lean proteins, and healthy fats—can significantly influence how our body responds to the sugar we intake. Furthermore, proper nutrition ensures that when we engage in physical activities, our body has the right fuel to perform optimally.

Consider a straightforward analogy: think of our body as a car. A car requires the right type of fuel to run efficiently. Similarly, our bodies need proper nutrition. But a car also needs to be driven regularly; keeping it stagnant isn't ideal. In the same way, our bodies need regular physical activity to keep all systems running smoothly. It's a symbiotic relationship where one component amplifies the benefits of the other.

Let's examine the journey of Mark, a 40-year-old diagnosed with Type 2 diabetes. Mark's initial approach to his diagnosis was primarily focused on medication. But soon, he realized the potential of integrating exercise and nutrition into his routine. Mark started by adjusting his diet. He prioritized whole foods, minimized processed sugars, and paid attention to portion sizes. To complement his improved diet, Mark incorporated a mix of cardiovascular exercises and strength training into his weekly routine. The changes didn't happen overnight. But over time, Mark noticed more stable blood sugar levels, improved energy, and better overall health.

Mark's story underscores the idea that managing diabetes isn't just about medication. It's about a holistic approach where lifestyle plays a crucial role. He learned that the combination of a well-balanced diet and regular exercise could offer him better control over his condition than either aspect could alone.

So for anyone grappling with Type 2 diabetes or aiming for better health in general, the key is integrating both physical activity and solid dietary habits. This dual approach doesn't just offer better control over blood sugar levels but fosters a sense of well-being, stamina, and vitality. The choices we make daily regarding our food and activity can dictate the trajectory of our health in the long run. With the right decisions, we can steer our journey towards a healthier and more fulfilling life.

Long-term Benefits of Proper Nutrition

Have you ever contemplated the elegance of a well-tuned instrument? Each chord resonates with such purity and precision that it caresses the very soul. It's not just the strings or the wood that crafts this music, but the dedication of time and care. Similarly, the human body, a magnificent orchestra of cells, tissues, and organs, thrives on the melodies of proper nutrition. Beyond the immediate satiation of hunger or the fleeting joys of taste, lies a world where the music of health and well-being plays ceaselessly, crafting our story.

Picture, for a moment, a grand oak tree. Mighty, tall, and deeply rooted. Its grandeur didn't come about overnight. Seasons changed, winds blew, rains poured, yet the oak stood firm, drawing sustenance from the earth, turning the very challenges of its environment into pillars of its strength. This is the magic of nutrition. Much like that grand oak, we too are the sum total of what we feed our bodies over years, if not decades.

The whispers of immediate benefits from a balanced meal—like feeling full, energetic, or that radiant glow on one's skin—are but the tip of the iceberg. Dive deeper beneath the surface, and you'll find a treasure trove of long-term benefits that proper nutrition bestows upon us.

One of the most profound gifts of sustained nutritional mindfulness is the bolstering of our body's defense mechanisms. Just as a kingdom with robust walls and vigilant sentinels stands undeterred by invaders, our body, when nourished with the right nutrients, fortifies its defenses against a plethora of diseases. For instance, a diet rich in antioxidants, sourced from a colorful palette of fruits and vegetables, acts as a shield against the ravages of free radicals, which, left unchecked, could lead to degenerative diseases.

Moreover, consider the intricate highways and byways of our circulatory system. The heart, a tireless workhorse, pumps life into every corner of our body. By embracing heart-healthy foods—those low in saturated fats, devoid of trans fats, and replete with omega-3 fatty acids—we not only serenade our heart with love but also ensure it beats with youthful vigor, long into the twilight of our years.

Yet, the magic of nutrition isn't confined merely to the physical realm. It dances gracefully into the domain of the mind. Omega-3 fatty acids, found in abundance in fatty fish, walnuts, and flaxseeds, are not just friends of the heart but allies of the brain. They play a pivotal role in maintaining the health of neuron membranes. A well-nourished brain is a crucible of clarity, creativity, and cognitive longevity.

Let's embark on a little thought experiment. Imagine two individuals: Alex and Jamie. Alex, with a nonchalant approach to nutrition, finds solace in fast foods, sugary sodas, and processed snacks. Jamie, on the other hand, cherishes the symphony of nutrition, with meals crafted from whole grains, lean proteins, leafy greens, and a smorgasbord of fruits.

Over the years, while the immediate differences in their choices might appear subtle, the long-term contrast is stark. Alex, unfortunately, becomes acquainted with frequent doctor visits, battles lethargy, and grapples with the fog of an unfocused mind. Jamie, meanwhile, feels invigorated, even as the years advance. Climbing flights of stairs, enjoying long walks in nature, or diving into intellectually stimulating pursuits, Jamie's life is a testament to the power of proper nutrition.

Now, one might wonder, is it merely about evading ailments? The answer is a resonant "No!" Proper nutrition, in its sublime essence, is about elevating the quality of life. It's about feeling vibrant, alive, and pulsating with energy, not just today or tomorrow, but decades down the line. It's about aging gracefully, with the wisdom of the years etched on one's soul, but the vitality of youth coursing through one's veins.

There's a poetic beauty in understanding that the choices we make at the dining table today echo into the vast corridors of our future. They define not just our lifespan but our 'healthspan'. The aroma of freshly cooked quinoa, the crunch of almonds, the burst of flavors from a berry—all these are not just culinary experiences. They are life choices, affirmations of a future filled with vigor, zest, and well-being.

To conclude, in the grand tapestry of existence, threads of proper nutrition weave patterns of profound beauty and significance. It's an investment, not just in the present, but a commitment to a future where every note of life's song reverberates with health, harmony, and happiness. So, as we journey through the myriad flavors of existence, let's make choices that craft not just a melody for today, but a symphony for a lifetime.

Strategies to Maintain Motivation

The tango of life is a dance of highs and lows, crescendos and quietudes. Yet, when we talk about managing a condition like type 2 diabetes or merely embracing a healthier lifestyle, one element remains curiously elusive – motivation. A blazing fire one day, a flickering candle the next; motivation, in its mercurial essence, often becomes the Achilles' heel in our journey toward better health.

Picture yourself on the cusp of a new dawn, invigorated by a newfound knowledge of the power of nutrition, exercise, and positive habits. You're armed with the best advice, the most delectable healthy recipes, and a workout regime that promises results. But a few weeks, maybe months down the line, the initial zeal starts to wane. The call of the old ways, the allure of shortcuts, the comfort of the familiar all beckon. This is where the alchemy of maintaining motivation becomes paramount.

Firstly, let's dispel a myth. Motivation isn't a boundless wellspring but rather a garden that requires tending. And like any seasoned gardener will tell you, the key lies in consistent nurturing and occasional re-invention.

Crafting a Personal Narrative

We're all, in essence, storytellers. The tales we tell ourselves, about ourselves, often shape our choices. If you've always seen yourself as someone who 'hates exercise' or 'can't resist sweets,' it's time to rewrite that script. Start viewing yourself as the protagonist of your health journey. A hero doesn't lack challenges but overcomes them with determination and sometimes, a little ingenuity. Every choice that aligns with your health goals is a chapter in this inspiring saga. This isn't about vanity or hubris but an honest acknowledgment of your efforts.

Celebrate the Small Wins

A symphony is not just about the grand crescendos but also the gentle notes that bridge the music. Similarly, your health journey will be punctuated with milestones—some big, some small. Maybe it's choosing a salad over fries, or perhaps it's walking for an extra ten minutes. Celebrate these moments. They are affirmations of your commitment. And while a grand goal, like shedding a certain number of pounds, is essential, these little victories provide the daily fuel to keep the engine of motivation running.

Embrace the Power of Community

There's a certain magic in collective energy. Whether it's a fitness group, a nutrition workshop, or merely a friend who shares your health goals, having companions on this journey can be immensely invigorating. Sharing struggles, exchanging tips, or sometimes just the knowledge that you're not in this alone can act as a potent motivation booster.

Visual Cues and Affirmations

Human beings are inherently visual creatures. Having tangible reminders of why you started on this journey can be a powerful motivator. Maybe it's a picture from a time when you felt healthier, or perhaps it's a dream outfit you'd like to wear. Place these visual cues where you'll see them often. Accompany them with affirmations—positive, present-tense statements like "I am making choices that honor my health." These aren't just words; they're seeds of intention that you plant every day.

Understanding the 'Why'

At the heart of motivation lies the 'why.' Why did you choose this path? Was it to feel more energetic, to manage a health condition, or perhaps to be an example for someone you love? This 'why' is your compass. When the journey gets arduous, or distractions beckon, revisiting this core reason can provide clarity and reignite your motivation.

Flexible Adaptation

Flexibility is not about compromising on your goals but about understanding that the path isn't always linear. Maybe an injury prevents you from following your regular workout, or perhaps a holiday season tempts you with culinary indulgences. Instead of viewing these as setbacks, consider them as part of the journey. Adapt, recalibrate, and find alternate ways to stay aligned with your health objectives.

Knowledge as a Catalyst

The world of health and wellness is ever-evolving. New research, novel insights, and innovative techniques are continually emerging. Stay curious. The more you understand the profound impacts of your choices, the more tangible and immediate your goals become. Whether it's a book, a documentary, or an enlightening conversation, let knowledge be a continual source of inspiration.

In conclusion, the voyage to better health and managing conditions like type 2 diabetes is not a sprint but a marathon. It demands endurance, resilience, and a fair bit of heart. Motivation, in this context, is less about sporadic bursts of enthusiasm and more about a steady flame that illuminates the path. By tending to this flame, by understanding its nature and needs, you're not just moving forward; you're crafting a journey that's as enriching as the destination. Remember, every step taken with intention is a step closer to your vision of health, vitality, and a life brimming with possibilities.

Additional Resources and Tools for a Healthy, Diabetes-Free Life

In the majestic tapestry of life, every thread holds significance, every hue contributes to the final picture. This tapestry, when unraveled, reveals a universe teeming with tools and treasures waiting to be discovered. The journey to health, particularly in the context of warding off the specter of type 2 diabetes, is no different. It isn't confined to just the realms of nutrition and exercise; it's augmented by the many resources and tools that can serve as your steadfast allies in this odyssey.

Imagine, if you will, embarking on an enchanting forest hike. The trails are signposted, yet the vastness of the woods can be overwhelming. In this journey, the resources and tools are akin to a compass, a map, or even the lilting song of a bird guiding you home. Let's delve into these resources, these unsung harmonies that can make your journey to health more intuitive, more enlightening, and above all, more sustainable.

The Digital Avatars: Apps and Platforms

In an era where technology has woven itself into the very fabric of our lives, health and wellness have found their champions in a myriad of digital platforms. Applications that track blood sugar levels, chart out dietary needs, or even craft customized workout regimes are the modern-day wizards. They aren't just passive tools but interactive entities, evolving with your needs, celebrating your milestones, and even gently nudging you when you veer off track.

Consider, for instance, a young mother named Clara, who found herself on the precipice of type 2 diabetes. For Clara, remembering to monitor her blood sugar was a challenge amidst the chaos of daily life. Enter a nifty app, equipped with reminders, historical data, and even insights on patterns. This app didn't just serve as a tracker; it became Clara's digital confidante, her beacon in navigating the complexities of her condition.

Literature's Lighthouse: Books and Journals

The age-old allure of books, journals, and articles remains undiminished. They serve as windows to wisdom, gateways to knowledge garnered over eons. While digital tools provide real-time assistance, literature offers depth, context, and a tapestry of experiences. From understanding the science behind diabetes to relatable memoirs of those who've trodden the path, there's a universe of written resources awaiting your perusal.

Let's accompany Robert, a retired banker with a penchant for reading. As he grappled with the early signs of diabetes, his sanctuary was his study, lined with books. From understanding the glycemic index to deciphering the nuances of metabolism, his literary explorations fortified his real-world choices. The books, in essence, became his silent mentors.

The Healing Power of Communities

Beyond the tangible, there's an intangible, yet profoundly impactful resource – the community. Support groups, workshops, and even online forums can be transformative. These are sanctuaries of shared experiences, collective wisdom, and above all, the comforting knowledge that you aren't alone.

Delve into Maya's journey, for instance. A passionate baker, the diagnosis of prediabetes felt like a cruel irony. Yet, in a local support group, she found her tribe. Here, stories were exchanged, recipes reinvented, and challenges collectively overcome. It was more than just a group; it was a tapestry of hope, resilience, and shared purpose.

The Ancients' Wisdom: Alternative Therapies

While modern medicine offers a plethora of insights, sometimes, the whispers of ancient wisdom can provide unique perspectives. Be it the holistic approach of Ayurveda, the energy pathways of acupuncture, or the calming allure of meditation, these ancient arts offer tools that can complement your health journey.

For Daniel, a high-flying executive, stress was a constant companion. While his diet was immaculate and his fitness regime enviable, the cortisol storms threatened to derail his health. It was in the quietude of meditation and the balanced energies of acupuncture that he found his equilibrium.

The Evolving Landscape of Research

Science, in its ceaseless quest for truth, continually unravels new insights, techniques, and discoveries. Staying attuned to this evolving landscape can be an invaluable resource. Not in the sense of sporadically jumping from one trend to another, but in discerning and integrating genuine advancements into your health tapestry.

In essence, the journey to a diabetes-free life is like an intricate dance. It's a choreography that transcends the basics of diet and exercise, drawing from a vast reservoir of resources and tools. From the digital wonders of the modern age to the timeless wisdom of literature, from the collective embrace of communities to the profound depths of ancient therapies, and the ever-evolving annals of research, myriad allies await your discovery.

Remember, every resource, every tool, is like a note in the symphony of health. When played in harmony, they can craft a melody that resonates with vitality, vigor, and a vibrant life, free from the shackles of diabetes.

Risk Factors and Prevention: Painting a Future Free from the Shadows of Diabetes

In the vast tableau of human existence, where each choice weaves a unique thread into our life's story, certain choices cast shadows, shadows that can darken the vibrant colors of health and well-being. But as any artist knows, understanding the shadow is vital to crafting a masterpiece. In our journey of life, understanding the risk factors for type 2 diabetes becomes the brushstroke that enables us to paint a brighter, healthier future. Let us then journey into these shadows, not with trepidation, but with the resolve of an artist aiming to create a magnum opus.

A Whirlwind Named Genetics

Imagine a symphony, a continuous thread of music that began long before you were born and will continue long after. This symphony is your genetic code, an intricate composition passed down through generations. Each note, a gene, carries with it the tales of your ancestors, their strengths, vulnerabilities, triumphs, and tribulations. But what does this mean for type 2 diabetes?

Within this genetic symphony, certain melodies or patterns may predispose an individual to diabetes. These predispositions are not condemnations, but rather a predisposition, a subtle nudge towards a potential. Think of it as the wind nudging a dandelion's seeds; the seeds may float in that direction, but not all will take root. In similar fashion, while genetic markers might increase susceptibility to diabetes, environmental factors, lifestyle choices, and even sheer chance play significant roles in determining if the disease manifests. The key is to be attuned to this melody, to understand it, and to preemptively harmonize it with positive lifestyle choices.

The Silent Footsteps of Age

Like the relentless waves sculpting a shoreline, time etches its marks upon us. Age, with its wisdom and experiences, also brings physiological changes. As the years accumulate, so does the wear and tear on our body's machinery, including the intricate system that manages blood sugar.

The pancreas, the maestro in our body's insulin orchestra, can start to falter with age. The insulin it produces might not wield the same potency, or the body's cells might not respond to insulin's overtures as they once did, a condition known as insulin resistance. This evolving dynamic makes older adults more susceptible to elevated blood sugar levels. However, like a seasoned musician adjusting to a slightly out-of-tune instrument, we can recalibrate our lifestyles to this changing dynamic. While age's footsteps are silent, they needn't be stealthy; forewarned is forearmed.

The Labyrinth of Lifestyle

The modern world, with all its conveniences and comforts, has woven a complex maze around us. Skyscrapers reach for the heavens but often trap us in elevators. Technological marvels connect us globally while often disconnecting us from physical activity. This modern labyrinth, while dazzling, can lead us into sedentary traps.

Prolonged periods of inactivity can disrupt the metabolic processes, leading to weight gain and increased abdominal fat, both potent risk factors for diabetes. Moreover, the constant barrage of processed foods, high in sugars and unhealthy fats, acts like quicksand, pulling us deeper into the maze. But every labyrinth has an exit. Recognizing these pitfalls and making deliberate choices—like opting for stairs, taking frequent breaks from sitting, or choosing natural foods over processed ones—can guide us out of this maze.

The Intricate Ballet of Hormones

In the vast theater of our body, hormones dance gracefully, maintaining a delicate balance. Like ballet dancers, their moves are precise, timed to perfection, ensuring that everything from growth and mood to metabolism and blood sugar stays in harmony.

However, there are instances when this ballet is interrupted. Conditions such as polycystic ovary syndrome (PCOS) can throw off the hormonal balance, introducing higher levels of androgens, often termed "male hormones." This hormonal misstep can lead to insulin resistance. Similarly, disorders of the adrenal or pituitary glands might introduce unscripted moves in the hormonal ballet, escalating the risk of diabetes. But, like any grand performance, with the right interventions, guidance, and awareness, the dance can be realigned, and the ballet can regain its harmonious flow.

The Silent Echo of Gestational Diabetes

Pregnancy is akin to a celestial dance, where life is nurtured and a new star is born. However, sometimes, dark clouds of gestational diabetes can cast a shadow over this luminous journey. Gestational diabetes, while temporary, resonates like a silent echo long after the baby's birth. Women who experience this condition are more likely to develop type 2 diabetes later in life. The ripple effect of this diagnosis also extends to the child, predisposing them to potential weight issues or diabetes in the future. Yet, like an attentive meteorologist can predict and prepare for a storm, awareness, regular screenings, and proactive lifestyle measures can dispel these clouds, ensuring that the silent echo doesn't amplify over time.

The Vigil of Regular Check-ups

Sailors of old would constantly scan the horizon, vigilant for changes in the weather or the sight of land. Similarly, regular medical check-ups act as our personal horizon scans. They alert us to shifts in our body's landscape, capturing subtle signs before they burgeon into full-blown storms. These medical forays are essential, especially for conditions like diabetes, which often whisper before they roar. By maintaining this vigil, one can catch early indicators of insulin resistance or elevated blood sugar and embark on corrective courses, preventing potential complications.

The Symphony of Balanced Nutrition

In the grand orchestra of health, balanced nutrition plays the lead melody. Each food group contributes its unique note, harmonizing into a song of vitality. Carbohydrates set the rhythm, proteins build the harmony, and fats, when chosen wisely, provide the rich undertones. However, dissonance occurs when we indulge in excess sugars, trans fats, and overly processed foods. This dietary cacophony can strain our body's metabolic processes and insulin responses. Yet, with a discerning palate and informed choices, we can conduct this nutritional symphony with grace, ensuring that our body resonates with health and energy.

The Dance of Active Living

Our bodies are designed for movement, a beautiful choreography of muscles, bones, and joints. Active living is not about strenuous exercise alone, but a holistic embrace of mobility. From the gentle waltz of a morning walk to the energetic tango of a gym session, every step, stretch, and sway contributes to better blood sugar control, enhanced insulin sensitivity, and overall vitality. This dance strengthens our heart, fortifies our bones, and uplifts our spirits. By making movement an integral part of our daily sonnet, we ensure that our life's dance remains vibrant and spirited.

The Embrace of Healthy Weight

Carrying excessive weight, especially around the abdomen, is like shouldering a cumbersome burden that strains our body's systems. Beyond the gravitational pull, this weight impacts our metabolic functions, lipid profiles, and insulin dynamics. A healthy weight is not about adhering to societal beauty standards but about lightening this load and letting our body function with unburdened efficiency. This embrace is a celebration of self-love, where we nourish with purpose and move with joy, ensuring that our internal machinery runs smoothly, keeping diabetes and its cohorts at bay.

The Wisdom of Moderation

In the grand tapestry of life, moderation weaves a golden thread. It's the wisdom of savoring a treat without overindulgence, of relishing relaxation without lethargy, and of pursuing passions without burnout. With regards to health and diabetes prevention, moderation is the key that unlocks sustainable habits. It teaches us that it's alright to occasionally indulge, as long as we balance it with mindful choices elsewhere. By internalizing this wisdom, we build resilience, foster self-awareness, and cultivate a lifestyle where excesses don't sway us, and balance becomes our guiding star.

In conclusion, our life's canvas, kissed by choices and circumstances, narrates a unique story. While shadows like risk factors are inevitable, our brushstrokes of awareness and prevention can ensure that the final artwork, our health, remains a radiant masterpiece, untouched by the blight of diabetes. Remember, in the grand gallery of life, every individual has the potential to be both the artist and the masterpiece.

Index

Measurement conversion table

Measurement	Conversion
1 teaspoon (tsp)	5 milliliters (ml)
1 tablespoon (Tbsp)	15 milliliters (ml)
1 fluid ounce (fl oz)	30 milliliters (ml)
1 cup	240 milliliters (ml) / 8 fluid ounces (fl oz)
1 pint (pt)	2 cups / 480 milliliters (ml) / 16 fluid ounces (fl oz)
1 quart (qt)	2 pints (pt) / 32 fluid ounces (fl oz) / 0.946 liters (l)
1 gallon (gal)	4 quarts (qt) / 128 fluid ounces (fl oz) / 3.785 liters (l)
1 ounce (oz)	28.35 grams (g)
1 pound (lb)	16 ounces (oz) / 454 grams (g)
1 kilogram (kg)	2.204 pounds (lb) / 35.27 ounces (oz)

Temperature conversion table

Fahrenheit (°F)	Celsius (°C)
32°F	0°C
50°F	10°C
68°F	20°C
86°F	30°C
104°F	40°C
122°F	50°C
140°F	60°C
158°F	70°C
176°F	80°C
194°F	90°C
212°F	100°C